THE CRADLE SONG

Comedy in Two Acts
With an Interlude in Verse

BY

GREGORIO AND MARÍA MARTÍNEZ SIERRA

English Version by
JOHN GARRETT UNDERHILL

SAMUEL  FRENCH

LONDON
NEW YORK   TORONTO   SYDNEY   HOLLYWOOD

Copyright © 1915 by John Garrett Underhill
Copyright © 1917 by John Garrett Underhill
Copyright © 1922 by E. P. Durron & Co
Copyright © 1934 by Samuel French Ltd
All Rights Reserved

THE CRADLE SONG is fully protected under the copyright laws of the British Commonwealth, including Canada, the United States of America, and all other countries of the Copyright Union. All rights, including professional and amateur stage productions, recitation, lecturing, public reading, motion picture, radio broadcasting, television and the rights of translation into foreign languages are strictly reserved.

ISBN 978-0-573-01079-8

www.samuelfrench.co.uk
www.samuelfrench.com

FOR AMATEUR PRODUCTION ENQUIRIES

UNITED KINGDOM AND WORLD EXCLUDING NORTH AMERICA

plays@SamuelFrench-London.co.uk

020 7255 4302/01

Each title is subject to availability from Samuel French, depending upon country of performance.

CAUTION: Professional and amateur producers are hereby warned that THE CRADLE SONG is subject to a licensing fee. Publication of this play does not imply availability for performance. Both amateurs and professionals considering a production are strongly advised to apply to the appropriate agent before starting rehearsals, advertising, or booking a theatre. A licensing fee must be paid whether the title is presented for charity or gain and whether or not admission is charged.

The professional rights in this play are controlled by Samuel French Ltd, 52 Fitzroy Street, London, W1T 5JR.

No one shall make any changes in this title for the purpose of production. No part of this book may be reproduced, stored in a retrieval system, or transmitted in any form, by any means, now known or yet to be invented, including mechanical, electronic, photocopying, recording, videotaping, or otherwise, without the prior written permission of the publisher. No one shall upload this title, or part of this title, to any social media websites.

The right of John Garrett Underhill, Gregorio and Maria Martinez Sierra to be identified as authors of this work has been asserted in accordance with Section 77 of the Copyright, Designs and Patents Act 1988.

FOREWORD

"THE CRADLE SONG" was first performed at the *Teatro Lara*, Madrid, on the 21st of February, 1911. At the outset it was seen to be a wholly exceptional piece, one of the rare inspirations of the theatre. The run, inaugurated modestly, continued throughout the season, while a reprise opened the same house during the autumn. Since that time "The Cradle Song" has been done everywhere, translated into all the major languages, meeting invariably with the same instant, affectionate response. Within the past decade it has taken its place as an international classic, serene and enduring as the simple humanity and faith which lie at its heart.

Augustin Duncan introduced the play to the English-speaking stage at the Times Square Theatre, New York, February 28, 1921, meeting with artistic success. On November 2, 1926, it was acted at the Fortune Theatre, London, with Miss Gillian Scaife as Sister Joanna of the Cross, achieving a run of 109 performances. Eva Le Gallienne next brought her singularly fine and sensitive interpretation to the Civic Repertory Theatre, New York, January 24, 1927, where it has been given 167 times. Meanwhile a special company headed by Miss Mary Shaw travelled through the United States. Other notable performances are those of the Old Vic, Everyman, "Q" and Scala Theatres, London, the Playhouses at Oxford and Liverpool, and the Abbey Theatre, Dublin. The play has proved equally popular with Anglican and Catholic, while, favoured by its locale, it seems especially at home in institutions of the Dominican Order. From as far afield as Nairobi, East Africa, Singapore, Straits Settlements, and Hobart, Tasmania, audiences bear tribute to its spell. The longest recorded run of "The Cradle Song" has been that of the French production at the Théâtre des Champs Elysées, Paris, where it exceeded 300 nights.

The text as printed follows the prompt book of the Civic Repertory Theatre. Attention may be called to the *Notes Upon Direction and Performance*, together with the biographical sketch of the authors, both of which will be found appended at the close of the volume.

JOHN GARRETT UNDERHILL.

NEW YORK,
1 *May* 1934.

FORTUNE THEATRE, LONDON
TUESDAY, NOVEMBER 2ND, 1926
ANMER HALL
PRESENTS

THE CRADLE SONG
A Comedy in Two Acts
By GREGORIO AND MARÍA MARTÍNEZ SIERRA
Translated by J. GARRETT UNDERHILL

CHARACTERS
(In the order of their appearance)

SISTER SAGRARIO	*Joan Hill.*
SISTER MARCELLA	*Ivy Des Voeux.*
THE PRIORESS	*Barbara Everest.*
SISTER JOANNA OF THE CROSS	*Gillian Scaife.*
MISTRESS OF THE NOVICES	*Mary Lincoln.*
THE VICARESS	*Isobel Pargiter.*
SISTER TORNERA	*Esme Hubbard.*
SISTER INEZ	*Di Forbes.*
DOCTOR	*David Horne.*
SISTER MARÍA JESÚS	*Peggy Rae.*
POET (*in Interlude*)	*George Wansbrough.*
TERESA	*Natalie Moya.*
ANTONIO	*Christopher Oldham.*

MONITORS, LAY SISTERS and NUNS: *Joan Dilla, Minnie Mather, Winifred Willard, Mary Pargiter, Dorothy Edwards and Lillie Aston.*

ACT I.—A room opening upon the Cloister of a Convent of Enclosed Dominican Nuns.

(Eighteen years are supposed to elapse between Acts I and II.)

ACT II.—The Convent Parlour.

Produced by A. E. FILMER.

TO
JACINTO BENAVENTE

THE CRADLE SONG
ACT I

A room opening upon the cloister of a Convent of Enclosed Dominican Nuns. The walls are tinted soberly; the floor is tiled. Three arches at the rear. In the R. wall a large door with a wicket in it, leading to a passage communicating with the exterior. A grilled peephole for looking out. Above the door a bell which may be rung from the street. Beside the door an opening containing a revolving box, or wheel, on which objects may be placed and passed in from the outside without the recipient's being seen or a view of the interior disclosed. Not far from this wheel, a pine table stands against one of the piers of the cloister. Ancient paintings relieve the walls. Through the arches the cloister garden may be seen, with a well in the middle; also a number of fruit trees, some greenery and a few rose bushes. Beneath the arches, potted flowers—roses, carnations, sweet basil, herb Louisa and balsam apple—together with a number of wooden benches and rush-seated chairs, and three armchairs.

As the CURTAIN *rises the* PRIORESS *is discovered seated in the largest of the armchairs, and the* MISTRESS OF NOVICES *and the* VICARESS *in the smaller ones, the former on the* R., *the latter on the* L., *well to the front. The other* NUNS *are grouped about them, seated also. The novices,* SISTER MARCELLA, SISTER JOANNA OF THE CROSS, SISTER MARÍA JESÚS *and* SISTER SAGRARIO *stand somewhat to the* R., SISTER JOANNA OF THE CROSS *occupying the centre of the stage. The* LAY SISTER *and* SISTER TORNERA *remain standing by the table at the rear.*

It is broad daylight. The scene is one of cheerfulness and animation.

SISTER SAGRARIO. Yes, do! Do! Do let her read them!
SISTER MARCELLA. Yes, do, Mother! Do say yes!
PRIORESS. Very well. You may read them, since you have written them.
SISTER JOANNA OF THE CROSS. I am very much ashamed.
MISTRESS OF NOVICES. These are the temptations of self-love, my child.
VICARESS. And the first sin in the world was pride.
SISTER JOANNA OF THE CROSS. They are very bad. I know you will all laugh at me.
VICARESS. In that way we shall mortify your vanity.

MISTRESS OF NOVICES. Besides, as this is not a school, our Mother will only be concerned with their intention.

PRIORESS. Begin. And do not be afraid.

SISTER JOANNA OF THE CROSS (*reciting*). To our Beloved Mother on the day of her Blessed Saint—her birthday:

> Most reverend Mother,
> On this happy day
> Your daughters unite
> For your welfare to pray.
> We are the sheep
> Who under your care
> Are seeking out Heaven—
> The path that leads there.
> On one side the roses,
> On the other the thorn,
> On the top of the mountain
> Jesus of Mary born.
> To Jesus we pray
> Long years for your life,
> And of the Virgin Maria
> Freedom from strife;
> And may the years vie
> In good with each other,
> In holiness and joy,
> Our dearly loved Mother!

(*The* NUNS *applaud and all speak at once.*)

SOME. Good! Very good!

OTHERS. Oh, how pretty!

SISTER TORNERA. They are like the Jewels of the Virgin!

SISTER INEZ (*depreciatively*). She has copied them out of a book.

SISTER JOANNA OF THE CROSS (*carried away by her triumph*). Long live our Mother!

ALL (*enthusiastically*). Long live our Mother!

PRIORESS. Come, you must not flatter me, my children. The verses are very pretty. Many thanks, my daughter. I did not know that we had a poet in the house. You must copy them out for me on a piece of paper, so that I may have them to read.

SISTER JOANNA OF THE CROSS. They are copied already, reverend Mother. If your Reverence will be pleased to accept them—— (*She offers her a roll of parchment, tied elaborately with blue ribbons. The verses are written on the parchment and embellished with a border of flowers, doves and hearts, all of which have been painted by hand.*)

PRIORESS (*taking and unrolling the parchment*). Bless me! What clear writing and what a beautiful border! Can you paint too?

SISTER JOANNA OF THE CROSS. No, reverend Mother. Sister María Jesús copied out the verses, and Sister Sagrario painted the border. Sister Marcella tied the bows.

SISTER MARCELLA. So it is a remembrance from all the novices.
PRIORESS. And all the while I knew nothing about it! The children have learned how to dissimulate very skilfully.
SISTER JOANNA OF THE CROSS. We had permission from Mother Anna Saint Francis. She gave us the ribbon and the parchment.
PRIORESS. No wonder, then. So the Mother Mistress of Novices can also keep a secret?
MISTRESS OF NOVICES. Once—— Only for to-day——
SISTER JOANNA OF THE CROSS. To-day you must forgive everything.
PRIORESS (*smiling*). The fault is not a grave one.
VICARESS (*acridly*). Not unless it leads them to pride themselves upon their accomplishments. The blessed mother Santa Teresa de Jesús never permitted her daughters to do fancy work. Evil combats us where we least expect it, and ostentation is not becoming in a heart which has vowed itself to poverty and humility.
MISTRESS OF NOVICES. Glory be to God, Mother Vicaress, but why must your Reverence always be looking for five feet on the cat?

(SISTER MARCELLA *laughs flagrantly*.)

VICARESS. That laugh was most inopportune.
SISTER MARCELLA (*pretending repentance, but still continuing to laugh in spite of herself*). I beg your pardon, your Reverence. I didn't mean it. This sister has such temptations to laugh, and she can't help it.
VICARESS. Biting your tongue would help it.
SISTER MARCELLA. Don't you believe it, your Reverence. No indeed it wouldn't!
PRIORESS (*thinking it best to intervene*). Come, you must not answer back, my daughter. I have no wish to punish anyone to-day.
VICARESS (*muttering*). Nor any other day, for that matter!
PRIORESS (*aroused*). What does your Reverence mean by that, Mother Vicaress?
VICARESS (*very meekly*). What we all know, reverend Mother—that the patience of your Reverence is inexhaustible.
PRIORESS. Surely your Reverence is not sorry that it is so?
VICARESS (*belligerently*). Not upon my account, no. For, by the grace of God, I am able to fulfil my obligation and accommodate myself to the letter and spirit of our holy rule. But there are those who are otherwise, who, encouraged by leniency, may stumble and even fall——
PRIORESS. Has your Reverence anything definite in mind to say? If so, say it.
VICARESS. I have noticed for some time—and the Lord will absolve me of malice—that these " temptations to laugh " of which Sister Marcella speaks, have been abounding in this community; and these, taken with other manifestations of self-indulgence, not

any less effervescent, are signs of a certain relaxation of virtue and deportment.

PRIORESS. I hardly think we need trouble ourselves upon that account. Providence has been pleased of late to bring into our fold some tender lambs, and perhaps they do frisk a little sometimes in the pastures of the Lord. But the poor children mean no harm. Am I right in your opinion, Mother Mistress of Novices?

MISTRESS OF NOVICES. You are always right in my opinion, reverend Mother. *Gaudeamus autem in Domino!*

VICARESS. Your Reverences of course know what you are doing. I have complied with my obligation.

(*The bell rings at the entrance.* SISTER TORNERA, *who is an active little old woman, goes up to the grille and looks through it, after first having made a reverence to the* PRIORESS.)

SISTER TORNERA. *Ave Maria Purissima!*

A VOICE (*outside, hoarse and rough*). Conceived without sin. Is it permitted to speak with the Mother Abbess?

SISTER TORNERA. Say what you have need of, brother.

VOICE. Then here's a present for her from my lady, the mayor's wife, who wishes her happiness, and sends her this present, and she's sorry she can't come to tell her herself; but she can't, and you know the reason.

(*The* PRIORESS *sighs, lifting up her eyes to heaven, and the others do the same, all sighing in unison.*)

And even if she could on that account, she couldn't, because she's sick in bed, and you know the reason.

SISTER TORNERA. God's will be done! Can the poor woman get no rest? Tell her that we will send her a jar of ointment in the name of the blessed Saint Clara, and say that these poor sisters never forget her in their prayers. They pray every day that the Lord will send her comfort. (*She turns the wheel by the grille, and a basket appears, neatly covered with a white cloth.*) Ah!—and the reverend Mother thanks her for this remembrance. And may God be with you, brother. (*Approaching the others with the basket, which she has taken from the wheel.*) Poor lady! What tribulations our Lord sends into this world upon the cross of matrimony!

PRIORESS. And to her more than anybody. Such a submissive creature, and married to a perfect prodigal!

MISTRESS OF NOVICES. Now that we are on the subject, your Reverences, and have the pot by the handle, as it were, do your Reverences know that the blasphemies of that man have completely turned his head? You heard the bells of the parish church ringing at noon yesterday? Well, that was because the mayor ordered them to be rung, because in the election at Madrid yesterday the republicans had the majority.

ALL. God bless us! God bless us!

Act I.]   THE CRADLE SONG.   13

VICARESS. Did the priest give his consent to that?

SISTER INEZ. The priest is another sheep of the same colour—he belongs to the same flock, may the Lord forgive me if I lack charity! Didn't your Reverences hear the sacrilege he committed upon our poor chaplain, who is holier than God's bread? Well, he told him that he was more liberal than the mayor, and that the next thing he knew, when he least expected it, he was going to sing the introitus to the mass to the music of the Hymn of Riego!

PRIORESS. Stop! Enough! It is not right to repeat such blasphemies.

MISTRESS OF NOVICES. Yes, calumnies invented by unbelievers, the evil-minded——

SISTER INEZ. No such thing! Didn't Father Calixtus tell me himself while he was dressing for mass this morning? We'll have to put a new strip down the middle of his chasuble quite soon.

PRIORESS. What? Again?

SISTER INEZ. Yes. It's all worn out; it looks terrible! Poor Father Calixtus is so eloquent! He tears the silk to ribbons, pounding his chest all the time.

VICARESS. God's will be done, the man is a saint!

PRIORESS. And all this while we have been forgetting the present from the mayor's wife. Bring it nearer, Sister.

SISTER SAGRARIO. Mercy! What a big basket!

SISTER TORNERA. It's very light, though.

SISTER MARÍA JESÚS. Perhaps it is sweetmeats.

SISTER INEZ. Ha! It's easy to see which sister has a sweet tooth!

SISTER MARÍA JESÚS (*aside*). As if she didn't like sweets!

SISTER MARCELLA. Now, Sister Inez, what did we see you doing this morning? You know we caught you licking the cake pan yourself.

SISTER INEZ. I? Licking the pan? Your Sister licking the pan? Oh, what a slander! *Jesús!*

PRIORESS. Come, you must not be displeased, Sister Inez; for it was said only in pleasantry. Ah, Sister Marcella! Sister Marcella! Do have a little more circumspection and beg your Sister's pardon.

SISTER MARCELLA (*kneeling before* SISTER INEZ). Pardon me, Sister, as may God pardon you, and give me your hand to kiss as a penance for having offended you.

PRIORESS. That is the way my children should behave, humbly and with contrition. Sister Inez, give Sister Marcella your hand to kiss, since she begs it of you so humbly.

SISTER MARCELLA (*spitefully, after kissing her hand*). Ay! But what a smell of vanilla you have on your fingers, Sister! Lovely! We're going to have tarts for dinner.

(*The others laugh.*)

SISTER INEZ (*irritated, almost in tears*). Vanilla? God-a-mercy! Vanilla! Look at me! Do my fingers smell of vanilla?

PRIORESS (*imposing silence*). Surely the devil must be in you, Sister Marcella, and may God forgive you for it! Go and kneel in the corner there, with your face to the wall, and make the cross with your arms while you repeat a greater station. May the Lord forgive you for it!

SISTER MARCELLA. Willingly, reverend Mother.

SISTER INEZ (*rubbing her hands under her scapular*). Too bad! Too bad! Ay! Ay! Ay!

SISTER MARCELLA (*aside*). Old box of bones! (*She goes and kneels in the corner, R., but keeps smiling and turning her head while she lets herself sink back on her heels, as if not taking the penance too seriously.*)

PRIORESS. You may uncover the basket now, Sister. Let us see what is in it.

SISTER TORNERA. With your permission, reverend Mother. Why! It's a cage!

SISTER SAGRARIO. With a canary in it!

ALL. A canary! A canary! Why, so it is! Let me see! How lovely!

MISTRESS OF NOVICES. Isn't it pretty?

SISTER MARÍA JESÚS. The dear! Isn't it adorable?

SISTER JOANNA OF THE CROSS. It looks as if it were made of silk.

SISTER INEZ. I wonder if it can sing?

PRIORESS. Of course it can sing. The mayor's wife would never send us a canary that couldn't sing.

SISTER SAGRARIO. What a beautiful cage! Why, there's a scroll on the front!

MISTRESS OF NOVICES. That isn't a scroll. It has letters on it.

SISTER MARÍA JESÚS. Why, so it has! Look and see what they say.

MISTRESS OF NOVICES (*reads*). "The Convent of Dominican Nuns!"

SISTER INEZ (*laughing*). I'd call that rather an airy convent!

VICARESS. That good woman is holier than God's bread.

PRIORESS. She could not have sent me anything that would have pleased me better. I have always been anxious to have a canary.

SISTER INEZ. The Carmelite Sisters have two lovely canaries, and they say last year on Holy Thursday they hung them in the door of the tomb they have in the church for Easter, and it was like a miracle to hear them sing.

MISTRESS OF NOVICES. Then, if ours sings, we can hang him in the church this year, and take the music box away.

PRIORESS. No, for the music box is a present from the chaplain, and he would be rightly offended. We will have the box and the canary there together, and when we wind up the box it will encourage the bird to sing.

Sister Joanna of the Cross. Oh, look at him now—he's taking his bath!
Sister Sagrario. See how he jumps.
Prioress. What wonders God performs!
Vicaress. And yet there are misguided creatures who pretend that the world made itself!
Sister Inez. Sister Marcella stuck her tongue out at me.
Sister Marcella. Oh, reverend Mother! I did nothing of the kind!
Vicaress. How nothing of the kind? Didn't I see it with my own eyes? And I was struck dumb!
Sister Marcella. I said I never stuck my tongue out at Sister Inez. I stuck it out because there was a fly on the end of my nose, and since I had my arms out making the cross, I had to frighten him away with something.
Sister Joanna of the Cross. Reverend Mother, since this is your Saint's day, won't you please excuse Sister Marcella this time?
Sister María Jesús. Yes, reverend Mother! I am sure she won't do anything that's wrong again.
Prioress. Sister Inez is the one who has been offended, and she is the only one who has the right to request her pardon.
Novices. She does! She does! You do, don't you, Sister Inez?
Sister Inez (*with a wry face*). Your Reverence will pardon her when your Reverence thinks best.
Prioress. Then come here, my erring daughter. She knows that I pardon her because of the day, and so as not to spoil the pleasure of her sisters.
Sister Marcella. May God reward you, reverend Mother!
Prioress. And set your veil straight, for this is the Lord's house, and it looks as if you were going on an excursion. And now to your cells, every one. (*To the* Novices.) What are you whispering about?
Sister Sagrario. We wanted to ask you something.
Sister María Jesús. And we are afraid to do it.
Prioress. Is it as bad as that?
Sister María Jesús. No, it isn't bad. But——
Sister Joanna of the Cross. Your Reverence might think so.
Prioress. I might? I am not so evil-minded.
Sister Sagrario. I—— I—— Our Mother Mistress will tell you.
Mistress of Novices. They mean me. Do you want me to?
Novices. Yes! Yes! Do!
Mistress of Novices. With God's help I will try. I am not sure, but I think they want to have your Reverence's permission to talk while they are waiting for the *fiesta* to begin. Am I right?
Novices. Yes! Yes! You are! Please, Mother, please!

SISTER MARCELLA. Long live our Mother!
PRIORESS. Silence! Silence! What? Haven't they had talking enough to-day after the dispensation I allowed them this morning?
VICARESS. The appetite always grows by what it feeds on. It is an unruly monster, and woe to her who gives it rein. If they came under my authority, I would not give them opportunity to make a single slip, for the holy Apostle Saint James has said and well said: " He who saith that he hath not offended by his tongue, lies."
SISTER MARCELLA. Ah, Sister Crucifixion! Don't spoil this holiday for our Mother.
VICARESS. Spoil it, eh? Who pays any attention to what I say in this house?
PRIORESS. Will you promise not to whisper nor offend the Lord with foolish talk?
NOVICES. We promise.
PRIORESS. Then you may talk as much as you like until the hour for prayers.
NOVICES. Thanks, thanks!

(*The bell rings at the entrance twice.*)

SISTER TORNERA. Two rings! The doctor!
PRIORESS. Cover your faces.

(*The* NUNS *lower their veils over their faces.*)

And pass out through the cloister.

(*The* NUNS *begin to file out slowly and disappear through the cloister.*)

SISTER SAGRARIO (*approaching the* PRIORESS). This Sister has a felon, reverend Mother.
PRIORESS. Remain, then—and you too, Sister María Jesús. (*To* SISTER TORNERA.) Open, Sister.

(*The* PRIORESS, SISTER TORNERA, SISTER SAGRARIO *and* SISTER MARÍA JESÚS *remain.* SISTER TORNERA *unchains, unbolts and opens the door. The* DOCTOR *enters. He is about sixty years of age.*)

SISTER TORNERA. Ave Maria Purissima!
DOCTOR. Conceived without sin. (*He comes in.*) Good morning, Sister.
SISTER TORNERA. Good morning, Doctor.
DOCTOR. Well, what progress are we making in holiness to-day?
SISTER TORNERA (*laughing*). Ho, ho, Doctor!
DOCTOR. Enough! Enough! No doubt, no doubt! (*Discovering the* PRIORESS.) Congratulations, Mother.
PRIORESS. What? A heretic, and yet you remember the days of the saints?
DOCTOR. You are the saint, Mother; you are the saint.

PRIORESS. Ah! You must not scandalize me before my novices.
DOCTOR. Novices? Where, where? I said so when I came in. I smell fresh meat.
PRIORESS. Don José! Don José!
DOCTOR. But I say no more. Come! To work! To work! What is the trouble with these white lambs?
SISTER SAGRARIO. Your handmaid has a felon, Doctor.
DOCTOR. Eh? On the hand? And such a lovely hand! Well, we shall have to lance it, Sister.
SISTER SAGRARIO (*alarmed*). What? Not now?
DOCTOR. No, to-morrow, Sister. To-morrow, unless it yields first to a poultice and five *Pater nosters*. Remember, not one less!
SISTER SAGRARIO (*in perfect earnest*). No, Doctor.
DOCTOR. And this other one, eh?
PRIORESS. Ah, Doctor! She has been giving me a great deal of worry. She falls asleep in the choir; she sighs continually without being able to give any reason; she cries without cause and has no appetite for anything but salads.
DOCTOR. How old are you?
SISTER MARÍA JESÚS. Eighteen.
DOCTOR. How long have you been in this holy house?
SISTER MARÍA JESÚS. Two years and a half.
DOCTOR. And how many more do you remain before you come to profession?
SISTER MARÍA JESÚS. Two and a half more, if the Lord should be pleased to grant this unworthy novice grace to become His bride.
DOCTOR. Let me see the face.
PRIORESS. Lift your veil.

(SISTER MARÍA JESÚS *lifts her veil.*)

DOCTOR. Hm! The Lord has not bad taste. A little pale, but well rounded, well rounded.
SISTER TORNERA. Don José! Who ever heard of such a doctor?
DOCTOR. So, we have melancholy; then, a constant disposition to sigh, combined with loss of appetite. Well, there is nothing else for it, Sister: a cold bath every morning and afterwards a few minutes' exercise in the garden.
SISTER TORNERA (*somewhat horrified*). Exercise? Don José!
DOCTOR. Unless we write home at once and tell her mother to come and fetch her and find the child a good husband.
SISTER MARÍA JESÚS. Oh, Don José! But this Sister has taken her vows to the Church!
DOCTOR. Well, in that case cold water. There is nothing else for it. For melancholy at eighteen, matrimony or cold water.
SISTER SAGRARIO (*summoning her courage*). As you always talk so much about it, Doctor, why don't you get married yourself?
DOCTOR. Because I am sixty, daughter; and it is fifteen years

since I have felt melancholy. Besides, whom do you expect me to marry when all the pretty girls go into convents?

PRIORESS. Doctor, Doctor! This conversation will become displeasing to me.

DOCTOR. Is this all the walking infirmary?

SISTER TORNERA. Yes, Doctor.

DOCTOR. And the invalid? How is she?

SISTER TORNERA. She is the same to-day, Doctor. Poor Sister Maria of Consolation hasn't closed her eyes all night! Don't you remember? Yesterday she said she felt as if she had a viper gnawing at her vitals? Well, to-day she has a frog in her throat.

DOCTOR. Goodness gracious! Come, let me see, let me see. What a continual war the devil does wage against these poor sisters! Long life, Mother, and happy days!

PRIORESS. Long life to you, Doctor. (*To* SISTER TORNERA.) Go with him, Sister, and meanwhile these children will take care of the gate.

(SISTER TORNERA *takes a bell from the table and, her veil covering her face, precedes the* DOCTOR *through the cloister, ringing solemnly in warning. They disappear.*)

I must withdraw to the choir; I fear that to-day I have fallen behind in devotion and prayer.

SISTER MARÍA JESÚS. Will your Reverence give us permission to call the others?

PRIORESS. Yes, call them; but be careful that you commit no frivolity.

(*The* PRIORESS *goes out.*)

SISTER MARÍA JESÚS (*approaching one of the arches of the cloister*). Sister Marcella! Sister Joanna of the Cross! Pst! Come out! We are watching the grille and we have permission to talk.

(SISTER MARCELLA *and* SISTER JOANNA OF THE CROSS *re-enter.*)

SISTER SAGRARIO. What shall we talk about?

SISTER JOANNA OF THE CROSS. Let Sister Marcella tell us a story.

SISTER MARCELLA. Yes, so that you'll all be shocked.

SISTER MARÍA JESÚS. *Ay!* We are not such hypocrites as that, Sister.

SISTER MARCELLA. Or so that Sister Sagrario can run and tell the Mother Mistress.

SISTER SAGRARIO. Oh, thank you, Sister!

SISTER MARCELLA. It wouldn't be the first time, either.

SISTER SAGRARIO. You needn't mind me, Sisters. I am going to sit here in the corner and work, and you can talk about whatever you please. I shan't hear you. (*She takes a pair of pincers, some beads and a piece of wire out of her pocket, and sitting down in a corner, begins to string a rosary.*)

SISTER JOANNA OF THE CROSS. Oh, come on, Sister! Don't be foolish.

(*They all surround her, and finally she allows herself to be persuaded, after many expressions of protest, like a small child who says, "I won't play."*)

SISTER SAGRARIO. Why! If they haven't forgotten the canary!

SISTER MARCELLA. Poor thing! How do you like to be left in this nest of silly women, little fellow? Let's open the cage.

SISTER MARÍA JESÚS. What for?

SISTER MARCELLA. So that he can fly away, silly, if he wants to.

SISTER SAGRARIO. No, no!

SISTER MARÍA JESÚS. Our Mother wouldn't like that.

SISTER MARCELLA. He would like it, though. Come on! (*She opens the door of the cage.*) Fly out, sweetheart! Fly away, the world is yours. You are free!

SISTER JOANNA OF THE CROSS. He doesn't fly out.

SISTER MARÍA JESÚS. He doesn't budge.

SISTER MARCELLA. Stupid, don't you see what a bright, sunny day it is?

SISTER JOANNA OF THE CROSS. They say canaries are born in cages and, see, now he doesn't care to fly away.

SISTER MARÍA JESÚS. He'd rather stay shut up all his life like us nuns.

SISTER MARCELLA. Then you're a great fool, birdie. (*She shuts the door of the cage.*) God made the air for wings and He made wings to fly with. While he might be soaring away above the clouds, he is satisfied to stay here all day shut up in his cage, hopping between two sticks and leaf of lettuce! What sense is there in a bird? *Ay*, Mother! And what wouldn't I give to be a bird!

SISTER JOANNA OF THE CROSS. Yes! What wouldn't you give to be a bird?

SISTER MARÍA JESÚS. They say that the swallows fly away every year over the ocean, and nobody knows where they go.

SISTER SAGRARIO. I often dream that I am flying in the night time—that is, not flying, but floating—just floating in the air without wings.

SISTER SAGRARIO. I often dream that I am running fast—oh, so fast!—and that I am skipping down stairs, without ever touching the ground or the stairs with my feet.

SISTER SAGRARIO. Isn't it nice? And how disappointed you are when you wake up and find that it was only a dream!

SISTER MARCELLA. I have dreamed that dream so many times that now, when I wake up, I hardly know whether it is a dream or reality.

SISTER JOANNA OF THE CROSS. What do you suppose it is that makes you dream the same dream so many times?

SISTER MARCELLA. I don't know, unless it is because it is the things you want to do, and you can't, and so you do them in dreams.
SISTER MARÍA JESÚS. What nice things you want to do!
SISTER SAGRARIO. But then what good would it be if you could do them? For instance, if we had wings like birds, where would we fly?
SISTER MARCELLA. I? I would fly to the end of the world!
SISTER MARÍA JESÚS. I? To the Holy Land, to Mount Calvary!
SISTER JOANNA OF THE CROSS. I would fly to Bethlehem and to the Garden of Nazareth, where the Virgin lived with the Child.
SISTER SAGRARIO. How do you know that there is a garden at Nazareth?
SISTER JOANNA OF THE CROSS. Of course there's a garden there, with a brook running by it. The song says so:

"The Virgin washed His garments
And hung them on the rose.
The little angels sing
And the water onward flows"——

(*Simply.*) And we had a garden by our house in the village, with a big rosebush at the edge of the brook that ran by it; and I used to kneel there and sing that song while I washed my baby brother's clothes, for there were seven of us children and I was the eldest. (*Feelingly.*) And that's what I miss most! (*Drying her eyes with her hands.*) Ay, Mother! And I always cry when I think of that baby boy! But it isn't right, I know. He loved me more than he did Mother, and the day that they took me away to the Convent, and I left home, he cried—he cried so that he nearly broke his little baby heart!

SISTER MARCELLA. I have a brother and a sister, but they are both older than I am. My sister married two years ago, and now she has a baby. (*With an air of importance.*) She brought him here once to show me.

SISTER JOANNA OF THE CROSS (*interrupting her, greatly interested*). I remember. He stuck his little hand in through the grille and your sister kissed it. Did you ever think how soft babies' hands are? Whenever I take communion I try to think I am receiving our Lord as a little child, and I take and press Him like this to my heart, and then it seems to me that He is so little and so helpless that I can't refuse Him anything. And then I think that He is crying, and I pray to the Virgin to come and help me quiet Him. And if I wasn't ashamed, because I know you would all laugh at me, I'd croon to Him, and rock Him to sleep, singing Him baby songs.

(*The bell rings by the grille.*)

SISTER SAGRARIO. The bell! I wonder who it is?
SISTER JOANNA OF THE CROSS. Better ask. That's why they left us here.

SISTER MARÍA JESÚS. Who will? I won't. I'm afraid.
SISTER SAGRARIO. So am I.
SISTER MARCELLA. You're not usually so bashful, I must say. I'll ask, though I was the last to enter the house. (*Going up to the grille, she says in a timid voice:*) Ave Maria purissima!
(*A moment's silence.*)
No one answers.
SISTER JOANNA OF THE CROSS. Try again. Say it louder.
SISTER MARCELLA (*raising her voice*). Ave Maria purissima!
SISTER SAGRARIO. Nothing this time, either.
SISTER MARÍA JESÚS (*summoning her courage, in a high-pitched voice*). Ave Maria purissima!
(*Another silence. The* NOVICES *look at each other in surprise.*)
SISTER MARCELLA. It is very strange.
SISTER MARÍA JESÚS. It must be spirits.
SISTER SAGRARIO. Oh, I'm afraid!
SISTER JOANNA OF THE CROSS. Nonsense! It's some mischievous little boy who has rung the bell as a joke on his way home from school.
SISTER MARÍA JESÚS. Peep through the hole and see if anybody is there.
SISTER MARCELLA (*stooping down to look*). No, nobody. But it looks as if there was something on the wheel. Yes—there is!
SISTER JOANNA OF THE CROSS. Let me see! Can't you turn it? (*She turns the wheel, and a second basket appears, carefully covered with a white cloth like the first.*) A basket!
SISTER SAGRARIO. Another present for our Mother.
SISTER MARÍA JESÚS. Of course it is! And here's a paper tied to it.
SISTER JOANNA OF THE CROSS (*reading, but without unfolding the paper*). "For the Mother Prioress."
SISTER SAGRARIO. Didn't I tell you?
SISTER MARCELLA. Somebody wants to give her a surprise.
SISTER JOANNA OF THE CROSS. I wonder if it's Don Calixtus, the chaplain?
SISTER MARCELLA. Of course it is!
SISTER MARÍA JESÚS. Or perhaps it's the Doctor.
SISTER JOANNA OF THE CROSS. No. He was here just now and he didn't say anything about it.
SISTER SAGRARIO. All the same it might be from him. And he wants to keep it a secret.
SISTER MARÍA JESÚS. Let's take it off the wheel.
SISTER MARCELLA (*lifting and carrying it to the table*). We'd better put it here by the canary. How heavy it is!
SISTER SAGRARIO. I wonder what it can be?
SISTER MARCELLA. Let's lift the corner and see.
SISTER MARÍA JESÚS. No, for curiosity is a sin.

SISTER MARCELLA. What of it? Come on! Let's do it. Who will ever know? (*She lifts the corner of the cloth a little and starts back quickly with a sharp cry.*) Ay!!
SISTER JOANNA OF THE CROSS (*hurrying to look*). Jesús!
SISTER MARÍA JESÚS. Ave Maria! (*Looking too.*)
SISTER SAGRARIO (*following*). God bless us!

(*The Convent is aroused at the cry of* SISTER MARCELLA. *Presently the* PRIORESS, *the* VICARESS, *the* MISTRESS OF NOVICES *and the other* NUNS *enter from different directions.*)

PRIORESS. What is the matter? Who called out?
VICARESS. Who gave that shout?
MISTRESS OF NOVICES. Is anything wrong?

(*The four* NOVICES, *trembling, stand with their backs to the basket, their bodies hiding it completely.*)

VICARESS. It is easy to see it was Sister Marcella.
PRIORESS. What has happened? Speak! Why are you all standing in a row like statues?
MISTRESS OF NOVICES. Has anything happened to you?
SISTER JOANNA OF THE CROSS. No, reverend Mother, not to us; but——
SISTER MARÍA JESÚS. No, reverend Mother; it's——
SISTER MARCELLA. Someone rang the bell by the wheel—and we looked—and there was nobody there—and they left a basket—this basket—and—and your sister had the curiosity to undo it——
VICARESS. Naturally, you couldn't do otherwise.
SISTER MARCELLA. And it's——
PRIORESS. Well? What is it?
SISTER MARCELLA. It's—I—I think it would be better for your Reverence to look yourself.
PRIORESS. By all means! Let me see. (*She goes up to the basket and uncovers it.*) Ave Maria! (*In a hoarse whisper.*) A baby!
ALL (*variously affected*). A baby?

(*The* VICARESS, *horrified, crosses herself.*)

PRIORESS (*falling back*). Your Reverences may see for yourselves.

(*The* NUNS *hurry up to the basket and surround it.*)

VICARESS. Ave Maria! How can such an insignificant object be so pink?
MISTRESS OF NOVICES. It's asleep.
SISTER JOANNA OF THE CROSS. See it open its little hands!
SISTER MARÍA JESÚS. Why! It has hair under the edge of its cap!
SISTER SAGRARIO. It is like an angel!
VICARESS. A pretty angel for the Lord to send us.

SISTER JOANNA OF THE CROSS (*as if she had been personally offended*). Ay, Mother Vicaress! You mustn't say that.
PRIORESS (*tenderly*). Where do you come from, little one?
VICARESS. From some nice place, you may be sure.
PRIORESS. Who can tell, Mother? There is so much poverty in the world, so much distress.
VICARESS. There is so much vice, reverend Mother.
MISTRESS OF NOVICES. You say that there was nobody at the grille?
SISTER MARCELLA. Nobody; no, Mother. The bell rang; we answered—but there was nobody there.
SISTER SAGRARIO (*picking up the paper which has fallen on the floor*). Here is a paper which came with it.
PRIORESS (*taking the paper*). "For the Mother Prioress."
VICARESS. An appropriate present for your Reverence.
PRIORESS. Yes, it is a letter. (*She unfolds the paper and begins to read.*)

" Reverend Mother:
Forgive the liberty which a poor woman takes, trusting in your Grace's charity, of leaving at the grille this newborn babe. I, my lady, am one of those they call women of the street, and I assure you I am sorry for it; but this is the world, and you can't turn your back on it, and it costs as much to go down as it does to go up, and that is what I am writing to tell you, my lady. The truth is this little girl hasn't any father, that is to say it is the same as if she didn't have any, and I—who am her mother—I leave her here, although it costs me something to leave her; for although one is what one is, one isn't all bad, and I love her as much as any mother loves her baby, though she is the best lady in the land. But all the same, though she came into this world without being wanted by anyone, she doesn't deserve to be the daughter of the woman she is, above all, my lady, of her father, and I don't want her to have to blush for having been born the way she was, nor for having the mother she has, and to tell it to me to my face, and I pray you by everything you hold dear, my lady, that you will protect her and keep her with you in this holy house, and you won't send her to some orphanage or asylum, for I was brought up there myself, and I know what happens in them, although the sisters are kind—yes, they are—and have pity. And some day, when she grows up and she asks for her mother, you must tell her that the devil has carried her away, and I ask your pardon, for I must never show myself to her, nor see her again, nor give you any care nor trouble, so you can do this good work in peace, if you will do it, for I implore you again, my lady, that you will do it for the memory of your own dear mother, and God will reward you, and she will live in peace, and grow up as God wills, for what the eyes have not seen the heart cannot understand, my lady."

VICARESS. Bless us! *Ave Maria!*
MISTRESS OF NOVICES. Poor woman!
SISTER JOANNA OF THE CROSS. Baby dear! Darling baby!
VICARESS. What pretty mothers the Lord selects for His children!
PRIORESS. God moves in His own ways, Sister. God moves in His own ways.
SISTER INEZ. Is that all the letter says?
PRIORESS. What more could it say?

(*The* DOCTOR *and* SISTER TORNERA *have re-entered during the reading.*)

DOCTOR. Exactly. What more could it say?
PRIORESS. What do you think, Don José?
DOCTOR. I think that somebody has made you a very handsome present.
PRIORESS. But what are we going to do with it? Because this poor woman has put this little creature into our hands and I would willingly protect her, as she asks, and keep the child here with us——
NOVICES. Yes, yes, Mother! Do! Do!
MISTRESS OF NOVICES. Silence!
PRIORESS. But I don't know if we can—that is, if it is right, if it is according to law—for when we enter this holy rule, we renounce all our rights—and to adopt a child legally—I don't know whether it can be done. How does it seem to you?
DOCTOR. I agree with you. Legally, you have no right to maternity.
VICARESS. And even if we had, would it be proper for our children to be the offspring of ignominy and sin?
PRIORESS. I would not raise that question, reverend Mother, for the child is not responsible for the sin in which she was born, and her mother, in renouncing her motherhood, has bitterly paid the penalty.
VICARESS. Yes, it didn't cost her much to renounce it.
PRIORESS. Do we know, Mother? Do we know?
VICARESS. We can guess. It is easy enough to go scattering children about the world if all you have to do is leave them to be picked up afterwards by the first person who comes along.
DOCTOR. How easy it is might be a matter for discussion. There are aspects of it which are not so easy.
SISTER SAGRARIO. Oh! She's opened her mouth!
SISTER JOANNA OF THE CROSS. The little angel is hungry.
SISTER MARÍA JESÚS. She's sucking her thumb!
SISTER JOANNA OF THE CROSS. Make her take her thumb out of her mouth. She'll swallow too much and then she'll have a pain.
SISTER SAGRARIO. Don't suck your fingers, baby.
SISTER JOANNA OF THE CROSS. See how good she is! You stop her playing, and she doesn't cry.
PRIORESS. There is another thing we must consider. What are we to do for a nurse?

Sister Joanna of the Cross. The gardener's wife has a little boy she is nursing now.

Prioress. In that case I hardly think she would care to be responsible for two.

Sister Joanna of the Cross. But it won't be any trouble—she's so tiny! Besides, we can help her with cow's milk and a little pap. The milk will keep on the ice and we can clear it with a dash of tea.

Doctor. It is easy to see Sister Joanna of the Cross has had experience with children.

Sister Joanna of the Cross. Your handmaid has six little brothers and sister. Ah, reverend Mother! Give her to me to take care of and then you will see how strong she'll grow up.

Vicaress. Nothing else was needed to complete the demoralization of the Novices. You can see for yourselves how naturally they take to this dissipation.

Prioress. I want you to tell me frankly what you think—all of you.

(*All speak at once.*)

Mistress of Novices. Your Sister thinks, reverend Mother——
Sister Tornera. Your handmaid——
Sister Inez. It seems to me——
Prioress (*smiling*). But one at a time.
Sister Tornera. It is an angel which the Lord has sent us, and your Sister thinks that we ought to receive her like an angel, with open arms.

Mistress of Novices. Of course we ought. Suppose, your Reverences, it hadn't been a little girl, but—I don't know—some poor animal, a dog, a cat, or a dove, like the one which flew in here two years ago and fell wounded in the garden trying to get away from those butchers at the pigeon-traps. Wouldn't we have taken it in? Wouldn't we have cared for it? And wouldn't it have lived happy for ever afterward in its cage? Can we do less for a creature with a soul than we did for a bird?

Sister Tornera. We must have charity.

Vicaress. I am glad the Mother Mistress of Novices has brought up the incident of that bird, for it will absolve me from bringing it up, as it might seem, maliciously. It was against my advice that that creature was received into this house, and afterward we had good reason to regret it, with this one saying, "Yes, I caught him!" and that one, "No, I took care of him!" and another, "He opens his beak whenever I pass by!" and another, "See him flap his wings! He does it at me!"—vanities, sophistries, deceits all of them, snares of the devil continually! And if all this fuss was about a bird, what will happen to us with a child in the house? This one will have to dress it, that one will have to wash it, another will be boasting, "It *is* looking at me!" another that it's at her that it

googles most—— There is Sister Joanna of the Cross making faces at it already!
SISTER JOANNA OF THE CROSS. What did your Reverence say?
VICARESS. Dissipation and more dissipation! Your Reverences should remember that when we passed behind these bars we renounced for ever all personal, all selfish affection.
MISTRESS OF NOVICES. Is it selfish to give a poor foundling a little love?
VICARESS. It is for us. Our God is a jealous God. The Scriptures tell us so.
MISTRESS OF NOVICES. Bless us! Mercy me!
VICARESS. And this quite apart from other infractions of our order which such indulgence must involve. For example, your Reverences—and I among the first—take no account of the fact that at this very moment we are transgressing our rule. We are conversing with our faces unveiled in the presence of a man.
PRIORESS. That is true.
DOCTOR. Ladies, as far as I am concerned—— Take no account of me——
PRIORESS. No, Doctor, you are of no account. I beg your pardon, Don José; I hardly know what I am saying.—Your Reverence is right. Cover yourselves—that is, it makes no difference—— The harm has been done—only once—— But comply with your consciences——

(*The* VICARESS *covers her face. The others, hesitating, wait for the* PRIORESS, *who makes a movement to do so, but then desists. The* VICARESS, *when she is covered, cannot see that she has become the victim of the rest.*)

But where were we? I confess that my heart prompts me to keep the child.
VICARESS. The Doctor already has told us that we have no right to maternity.
MISTRESS OF NOVICES. But the child is God's child, and she is returning to her Father's mansion.
VICARESS. God has other mansions for His abandoned children.
SISTER JOANNA OF THE CROSS. Don't send her to the asylum!
SISTER SAGRARIO. No!
PRIORESS. Her mother entreats us.
VICARESS. Her mother is not her mother. She has abandoned her.
PRIORESS. She has not abandoned her. She has entrusted her to others who seemed worthier to undertake her keeping.
VICARESS. Unholy egotism!
MISTRESS OF NOVICES. Christian heroism!
VICARESS. So? We are coining phrases, are we? Is this a convent, or an illustrated weekly?
MISTRESS OF NOVICES. Some people find life difficult and thorny.

VICARESS. Yes, but it is not our place to examine the details, since by the grace of God we have been relieved from the temptations and the frailties of the world.

MISTRESS OF NOVICES. All the more, then, we ought to have compassion on those who have fallen by the way.

VICARESS. Compassion? Mere sentiment!

MISTRESS OF NOVICES. The veil of charity!

PRIORESS. Silence! And let us not begin by rending it, irritating ourselves and aggravating each other. Don José, I suppose this birth will have to be reported?

DOCTOR. It will, madam. To the Registrar.

SISTER JOANNA OF THE CROSS. But then they will take her away?

DOCTOR. If nobody wants her. But if you have made up your minds you would like to keep her, I think I can propose a solution.

PRIORESS. A solution that is legal?

DOCTOR. Perfectly. Thanks be to God I am a single man. Although I am no saint, at least the population of this country has not been increased by a single soul on my account. It is true that I have not a penny, but, like everyone else, I have a couple of family names. They are at the service of this little stranger, if they will be of use to her. She will have no father and no mother—I cannot help that—but she will have an honourable name.

PRIORESS. Do you mean to say——?

DOCTOR. That I am willing to adopt her; exactly—and to entrust her to your care, because my own house—— The fact is the hands of Doña Cecilia are a little rough for handling these tiny Dresden dolls, and perhaps I might prove a bit testy myself. The neighbours all say that the air grows blue if my coat rubs against me as I walk down the street.

(*All laugh.*)

Besides, I am sure Sister Crucifixion is better equipped for the robing of saints.

VICARESS. Doctor, God help us both!

DOCTOR. Is it agreed?

PRIORESS. God reward you for it! Yes, in spite of everything. We shall notify the Superior immediately. There is no need for the child to live in the cloister. She can remain with the gardener's wife until she has grown older, and enter here later when she has the discretion to do so. She has been entrusted to our hands, and it is our duty to take care of her—a duty of conscience.

DOCTOR. If I cannot be of further service, I will go. And I will speak to the Registrar.

PRIORESS. As you go, be so kind as to ask the gardener's wife to come in. We must see if she will take charge of the child and nurse her. And ask her to bring along some of her little boy's clothes.

SISTER JOANNA OF THE CROSS. Yes, for we shall have to make a change immediately.

SISTER SAGRARIO. Shall we?
VICARESS. Not a change, but a beginning.
DOCTOR. Good afternoon, ladies.
ALL. Good afternoon, Don José.

(*The* DOCTOR *goes out. A pause.*)

PRIORESS. Sisters, may God pardon us if we have acted in this with aught but the greatest purity of motive. I hope and pray that His grace will absolve us of offence, nor find us guilty of having loved too much one of His poor children. The child shall be brought up in the shadow of this house, for we may say that her guardian angel has delivered her at the door. From this hour forth we are all charged with the salvation of her soul. The Lord has entrusted us with an angel and we must give Him back a saint. Watch and pray.
ALL. Watch and pray. We will, reverend Mother.
PRIORESS. And now bring her to me, Sister Joanna of the Cross, for as yet I have hardly seen the child. (*Looking at the child.*) Lamb of God! Sleeping as quietly in her basket as if it were a cradle of pure gold! What is it that children see when they are asleep that brings to their faces an expression of such peace?
SISTER JOANNA OF THE CROSS. They see God and the Virgin Mary.
SISTER MARÍA JESÚS. Perhaps the angel who watches over them whispers in their ears and tells them about heaven.
PRIORESS. Who can say? But it is a comfort to the soul to see a child asleep.
SISTER MARÍA JESÚS. It makes you want to be a saint, reverend Mother.
SISTER SAGRARIO. Will your Reverence grant me permission to give her a kiss?
SISTER MARÍA JESÚS. Oh, no! For it hasn't been baptized yet, and it is a sin to kiss a heathen!
PRIORESS. She is right. We must send for the Chaplain and have her baptized immediately.
MISTRESS OF NOVICES. What shall we call her?
SISTER INEZ. Teresa, after our beloved Mother.
SISTER TORNERA. María of the Miracles.
SISTER SAGRARIO. Bienvenida.

(*A large bell rings outside.*)

PRIORESS. The summons to the choir! We can decide later. Let us go.

(*The* NUNS *file out slowly, looking at the child as they go.*)

Stay with her, Sister Joanna of the Cross—you understand children; and wait for the gardener's wife. Follow the devotions from where you are, and do not let your attention falter.

(*All the* NUNS *go out, except* SISTER JOANNA OF THE CROSS, *who bends over the basket; then sinks on her knees beside it. The choir is heard within, led by a single* NUN *in solo, the responses being made in chorus, in which* SISTER JOANNA OF THE CROSS *joins. While the* NUN *is leading,* SISTER JOANNA OF THE CROSS *talks and plays with the child; then she makes her responses with the others.*)

VOICE WITHIN. *In nomine Patri et Filio et Spiritui Sancto.*

(SISTER JOANNA OF THE CROSS *crosses herself and says with the other* NUNS :)

VOICES WITHIN AND SISTER JOANNA OF THE CROSS. *Amen!*
SISTER JOANNA OF THE CROSS (*to the child*). Pretty one! Pretty one!
VOICE WITHIN. *Deus in adjutorium meum intende.*
VOICES WITHIN AND SISTER JOANNA OF THE CROSS. *Domine ad adjuvandum me festina.*
SISTER JOANNA OF THE CROSS (*to the child*). Do you love me, sweetheart? Do you love me?
VOICE WITHIN. *Gloria Patri et Filio et Spiritui Sancto.*
VOICES WITHIN IN CHORUS. *Sicut erat in principio et nunc et semper et insecula seculorum. Amen! Alleluia!*

(*But this time* SISTER JOANNA OF THE CROSS *makes no response. Instead she bends over the basket, embracing the child passionately, oblivious of all else, and says :*)

SISTER JOANNA OF THE CROSS. Little one! Little one! Whom do you love?

CURTAIN.

INTERLUDE
Spoken by the Poet

You came to-night to listen to a play;
Instead into a convent you made way.
Singular hardihood ! Almost profanation !
What will a poet not do to create sensation ?
Pardon, good nuns, him who disturbs the rest
And troubles the serene quietude of your nest,
Kindling amid the shades of this chaste bower
The flame of love you have renounced and flower.
Nay ! Do not frown because I have said love,
For you must know, chaste brides of God above,
That which you have deemed charity and pity,
The act of mercy, clemency for the pretty,
Unfriended foundling fate has brought along,
Yearning of adoption and the cradle song,
No other is than love's fire, divine and human
Passion ever brooding in the heart of woman.

Ah, love of woman, by whose power we live,
Offend so often—but to see forgive !
Whence do you draw your grace but from above ?
Whence simply ? Simply from maternal love !
Yes, we are children, woman, in your arms ;
Your heart is bread, you soothe our wild alarms,
Like children give us the honey of your breast.
In a cradle always your lover sinks to rest
Although he prostitutes our grovelling flesh.
Mother if lover, mother if sister too,
Mother by pure essence, day long and night through,
Mother if you laugh, or if with us you cry,
In the core of being, in fibre and in mesh,
Every woman carries, so God has willed on high,
A baby in her bosom, sleeping eternally !

So being women, you are lovers, nuns ;
Despite the ceintured diamond which runs
Across your virgin shields, showing in your lives
How to be mothers without being wives.
And in this child of all, you have poured all
The honey of your souls, and blended all

The fire of the sun, all fragrance and all light,
The first sweet morning kiss, the last good-night,
Till all her being tenderness exhales,
Her heart the home of love and nightingales.
A hundred times a woman but no saint.
The nuns pray in the choir; outside her plaint
A song; her prayer, gay rippling laughter.
Mass and the May morning slip by, she running after
Or dreaming in the garden. The roses smell
So sweetly! No child this for the hermits' cell.
She loves Heaven, but in good company ;
And before the altar of the Virgin see
Her with a boy, ruddier than the candle's flame,
A smiling, bashful boy, who soon will grow
To be a strong man, learn to give a blow
And take one, conquer worlds and redress wrong,
Justice in his heart, and on his lips a song!
"The child is mad," they say. Ah! No such thing!
With her into the convent entered Spring.

*This then the simple story. The poet would
Have told it day by day, if well he could,
In shining glory. But the task were vain.
The glory of our daily lives is plain.
For life builds up itself in such a way,
The water runs so clear, so bright the day,
That time is lulled to sleep within these walls.
An age or moment? Which passes? Who recalls?
The wheel turns round, but no one notes the turn.
What matter if the sisters' locks that burn
With gold, in time to silvery grey have paled?
Their hoods conceal it. And the pinks have failed
In the cheeks, and the lilies on the brow.
There are no mirrors. The sisters then as now
May walk in the garden, believe it still is May.

Among these hours which softly slip away,
This timeless time, we shyly pause at that
In which there is most warmth, the concordat
Of youth and incense, breaking of the spring.
The years have passed, the child is ripening.
The curtain rises on a soul in flower,
And a love chapter claims us for an hour.
It is quiet afternoon, quiet breeding;
The nuns are sewing and their sister reading:

* The Interlude may commence here if the entire poem is considered too long for any particular performance.

ACT II

Parlour of a Convent.

At the rear, a grille with a double row of bars. A curtain of dark woollen cloth hangs over the grille and intercepts the view of the outer parlour, to which visitors are admitted. This is without decoration, and may be brightly illuminated at the proper moment from the garden. A number of oil paintings of saints hang upon the walls—all of them very old and showing black stains. With them a carved crucifix or large black wooden cross. A small window furnished with heavy curtains, which, when drawn, shut off the light completely, is cut in the wall of the inner parlour on either side of the grille, high up toward the ceiling. There is an arched doorway on the L. *A pine table, a carved armchair, two other armchairs, smaller chairs and benches, together with all the materials necessary for sewing, complete the furnishings of the inner parlour.*

The PRIORESS, *the* MISTRESS OF NOVICES, SISTERS INEZ *and* TORNERA, SISTER SAGRARIO, SISTER JOANNA OF THE CROSS, SISTER MARCELLA, SISTER MARÍA JESÚS *and the other* NUNS *are discovered upon the rise of the* CURTAIN. *Only the* VICARESS *is absent. All are seated, sewing, with the exception of* SISTER MARÍA JESÚS, *who stands to* L. *of the* PRIORESS'S *chair, reading. A bride's trousseau is spread out upon the table and chairs. It is embroidered elaborately, trimmed with lace and tied with blue silk ribbons. A new trunk stands against the wall on the* R., *the trays being distributed about the benches and upon the floor.*

Eighteen years have passed. It must be remembered that the NUNS *have changed in appearance, and those who were novices have now professed and have exchanged the white for the black veil.*

SISTER MARÍA JESÚS (*reading and intoning*). "The Treasury of Patience, the Meditations of an Afflicted Soul in the presence of its God."
SISTER MARCELLA (*sighing*). *Ay!*
SISTER MARÍA JESÚS (*reading*). "First Meditation: The Sorrows of an Unhappy Spirit, Submerged in a Sea of Woe."

(*Outside,* TERESA'S *voice is heard, singing gaily.*)

TERESA. "Come singing and bringing
Flowers from the field,
Flowers from the field,
Sweet gardens, to Mary.
Flowers you must yield
For Love's sanctuary!"

(*The reader stops, and smiling, glances in the direction of the window through which the voice is heard. The other* NUNS *smile also, complacently.*)

PRIORESS (*with affected severity*). The child interrupts us continually.

SISTER INEZ. And a day like to-day!

SISTER JOANNA OF THE CROSS (*sympathetically*). She sings like a lark.

MISTRESS OF NOVICES (*indulgently*). She is so young!

SISTER MARCELLA. *Ay*, Mother!

PRIORESS. Continue reading, Sister María Jesús.

SISTER MARÍA JESÚS (*reading*). "The Sorrows of an Unhappy Spirit, Submerged in a Sea of Woe. My God, O my God, save me, for every moment I die! Overwhelmed, I sink in the midst of this terrible storm. Every moment I am buffeted and borne down. I am sucked into the uttermost depths, and there is no health in me!"

TERESA (*singing*). "From the glory of your brightness,
Radiantly sweet,
O, let me stoop and bend me
To kiss your feet!
Let me stoop and bend me
To kiss your feet!"

(*Again the reader stops. The* NUNS *smile.*)

PRIORESS. Sister Sagrario, will you step out into the garden and ask the child not to sing? We are reading.

(SISTER SAGRARIO *goes out,* R., *after making the customary reverence.*)

Continue, Sister, continue.

SISTER MARÍA JESÚS (*reading*). "There is no health in me. I cannot support myself; I cannot resist the shock of the horrible onrushing waves."

TERESA (*singing*). "You too were happy, Mary,
Happy in His love,
Flowers of love and springtime
That bloom above!"

(*The song is broken off suddenly, as if the* NUN *had arrived and commanded* TERESA *to stop. A moment later, there is a sound of light laughter.*)

c

PRIORESS. It cannot be helped. (*Smiling.*) The child was born happy and she will die so. (*To the reader.*) Continue.
SISTER MARCELLA. *Ay*, Lady of Sorrows!
PRIORESS. But Sister Marcella, my daughter, why do you sigh like this? Are you unwell?
SISTER MARCELLA. No, reverend Mother. But your daughter has temptations to melancholy.
PRIORESS. The Lord protect and keep you. You know how it displeases me to see the shadow of melancholy enter this house.
SISTER MARCELLA (*making a reverence*). *Ay*, reverend Mother, pardon me and assign me some penance if I sin, but your daughter cannot help it.
PRIORESS. Who was thinking of sin? Go out into the garden and take a little sunshine, daughter; that is what you need.
SISTER MARCELLA. *Ay*, reverend Mother, you don't know what you say! For when your daughter sees the flowers in the garden, and the blue sky so bright above them, and the sun so beautiful overhead, then the temptation comes upon her to sigh more than ever. *Ay!*
PRIORESS. If that is the case, return to your seat and let us pray that it may cease. But do not let me hear you sigh again, for I do not want to send you to prison to brighten your spirit in solitary confinement.
SISTER MARCELLA. As your Reverence desires. (*Returning to her seat.*) *Ay*, my soul!

(*The* PRIORESS *raises her eyes to heaven in resignation.*)

A NUN. *Ay*, Blessed Virgin!
ANOTHER. *Ay, Jesús!*
PRIORESS (*somewhat ruffled*). What? Is this an epidemic? Now all that is needed is for us to start sighing in chorus. Remember that the Lord is to be served with joy and thanksgiving "*in hymnis et canticis.*" Joy, the second fruit of the Spirit, springs from love, the highest of them all.

(*A pause.* SISTER MARÍA JESÚS *reopens the book, and without waiting for the signal from the* PRIORESS, *resumes reading.*)

SISTER MARÍA JESÚS (*reading*). "I cannot resist the shock of the horrible onrushing waves. They break over me unceasingly; irresistibly they bear me down."
PRIORESS. Close the book, Sister María Jesús: alas, the blessed father who wrote it was also burdened with a melancholy spirit!

(SISTER MARÍA JESÚS *closes the book, makes a reverence and sits down to sew. The* MOTHER VICARESS *appears in the door on the* L., *accompanied solemnly by two other* NUNS.)

VICARESS (*greatly agitated*). Ave Maria Purissima!

ACT II.] THE CRADLE SONG. 35

PRIORESS. Conceived without sin.
VICARESS. Have I permission, reverend Mother?
PRIORESS. Enter and speak. (*Looking at her.*) If I am not mistaken, your Reverence is greatly disturbed.
VICARESS. You are not mistaken, reverend Mother. No, and I dare affirm it is not for a slight reason. Your Reverence will be the judge as to whether this is the time and place to confront a member of this community with a charge of *ipso facto*.
PRIORESS. Speak, if public knowledge of the fault will not make a scandal and cause offence.
VICARESS. In the opinion of your handmaid all cause of scandal will be avoided by looking the offence straight in the face.
PRIORESS. Speak, then.
VICARESS (*making a profound inclination*). I obey. Reverend Mother, while making the round of my inspection of the cells with these two monitors, as your Reverence has been pleased to command —(*the two* MONITORS *each make a reverence*) and coming to the cell of Sister Marcella—(*all the* NUNS *look at* SISTER MARCELLA, *who lowers her eyes*) I found under the mattress of the bed—in itself a suspicious circumstance and sufficient to constitute a sin—an object which should never be found in the hands of a religious, an object which, to say nothing of the sin against the rule of holy poverty which the private possession and concealment of any property whatever must presuppose, is by its very nature a root of perdition and an origin and source of evil.
PRIORESS. Conclude, Mother, in God's name! For you keep us in suspense. What is this object?
VICARESS. Disclose it, sister.

(*To one of the* MONITORS. *The* MONITOR *makes a reverence, and draws from her sleeve a piece of glass, covered on one side with quicksilver.*)

PRIORESS. A piece of looking-glass.
VICARESS. Exactly, a piece of looking-glass!

(*Horrified silence on the part of the community.*)

PRIORESS. What has Sister Marcella to say to this?
SISTER MARCELLA (*leaving her place and kneeling before the* PRIORESS). Mother, I confess my guilt and I beseech your pardon.
PRIORESS. Rise.

(SISTER MARCELLA *rises.*)

Unhappy woman! What was the use of this piece of glass?
VICARESS. To look at herself in it, and amuse herself with the sight of her beauty, thus offending her Maker with pride and vain glory, and the exhibition of her taste.
SISTER MARCELLA (*humbly*). No, reverend Mother; no!

VICARESS. Or else to dress herself up and prink herself, and make faces and grimaces such as they do on the streets these days.

(*The* VICARESS, *who has taken the mirror, looks at herself in it for a moment, then turns it hurriedly away.*)

SISTER MARCELLA. No, reverend Mother.
PRIORESS. For nothing, then? For nothing, then?
SISTER MARCELLA. For nothing evil. On the contrary——
VICARESS. Ha! Now I suppose we are going to hear that it is a virtue in a religious to have a glass!
SISTER MARCELLA. No, reverend Mother, it is not a virtue. But your Reverences know already that your sister suffers from temptations to melancholy.
VICARESS. Yes, yes——
SISTER MARCELLA. And when they seize upon her too strongly, they put it into her head to climb trees and run along the tops of walls, and jump over the fences in the garden, and to throw herself into the water of the fountain, and since your Sister knows that, in a religious, these—these——
VICARESS. These extravagances.
SISTER MARCELLA. Are unbecoming, your Sister catches a sunbeam in the mirror and makes it dance among the leaves and across the ceiling of her cell, and over the walls opposite, and so she consoles herself and imagines that it is a butterfly or a bird, and can go wherever it pleaseth.
VICARESS. It can, and stay there.
PRIORESS. For this fault, Sister Marcella—

(SISTER MARCELLA *kneels*)

which, although not a grievous sin, must be punished by the constitution of our rule, I assign you this penance. Before you retire to-night you are to repeat the psalm "*Quam dilecta*" four times. Rise, and return to your seat.

(SISTER MARCELLA *obeys, but before seating herself she makes a reverence before each of the* NUNS.)

(*To the* VICARESS.) You may be seated.

(*The* VICARESS *and the two* MONITORS *seat themselves. Three light knocks on the door. It is* TERESA, *who says :*)

TERESA. *Ave Maria Purissima!*
PRIORESS. Conceived without sin.
TERESA. May I come in?
PRIORESS. Come in.

(TERESA *enters. She is eighteen, very pretty, very sunny and very gay, with nothing about her to suggest the mystic or the religious. She is dressed simply in grey and wears a white apron. She has a flower in her hair, which is arranged modestly, and without an excess of curls or ornament.*)

PRIORESS. Where are you coming from in such a hurry? You are out of breath.

TERESA (*speaks always with the greatest simplicity, without affectation or pretence of any sort*). From dressing the altar of the Virgin.

PRIORESS. Did that put you out of breath?

TERESA. No, Mother. It's because I wanted it to be all in white to-day, and there weren't white flowers enough in the garden, so I had to climb up and cut some branches off the acacia.

MISTRESS OF NOVICES. Did you climb a tree?

TERESA. Yes, I climbed two; there weren't enough blossoms on one.

MISTRESS OF NOVICES. *Jesús!*

VICARESS. *Ave Maria!*

TERESA. I wish you could see the view from the top of the big acacia!

(SISTER MARCELLA'S *eyes open wide with envy.*)

VICARESS. Child, you have put yourself beyond the pale of God's mercy!

SISTER JOANNA OF THE CROSS. You might have fallen! It's too terrible to think of!

TERESA. Fallen? No, Mother. Why, I've climbed it a hundred times!

PRIORESS. Then you must not do it again.

MISTRESS OF NOVICES (*regretfully*). It is too late to forbid her now.

PRIORESS (*sorrowfully*). That is true.

SISTER INEZ. It is the last day she will dress the altar.

SISTER JOANNA OF THE CROSS. The very *last!*

TERESA. Ah, Mothers! You mustn't talk like this. Don't be sad.

VICARESS. No, we had better behave as you do, if that were not impossible on such a day; and yet you are laughing and behaving like one possessed!

PRIORESS. The Mother is right. A little more feeling to-day, daughter, a manner more subdued, would not have been out of place.

TERESA. You are right, reverend Mothers—you always are, in the holiness, which like a halo surrounds your reverend heads; but when a girl wants to laugh she wants to laugh, although, as Mother Anna Saint Francis says, it may be the solemnest day of her life.

MISTRESS OF NOVICES. It is a solemn day, a very solemn day. You are leaving this house in which you have passed eighteen years, with hardly a thought as to how you happened to be here. To-morrow, you will be your own mistress, and you will have upon your conscience the responsibilities of a wife.

VICARESS. Which, believe me, are not light. Men are selfish, fickle——

TERESA (*timidly*). Antonio is very good.

VICARESS. However good he may be, he is a man, and men are accustomed to command. They have been from the beginning of the world, and it has affected their character. And since you are very independent yourself, and like to have your own way——

TERESA. Yes, I know I have been spoiled, but now you will see how good I can be. Things will turn out all right.

SISTER JOANNA OF THE CROSS. Do you want to spoil the day for her?

TERESA. No, Mother—no; you won't spoil it, for I am very, very happy. You have all been so good to me!

VICARESS. Nonsense! No such thing.

TERESA. But it isn't nonsense. I know this is God's house, but you might have closed the doors to me, and you have flung them wide open, freely. I have lived here eighteen years and in all this time, to the very moment that I am leaving it, you have never once reminded me that I have lived here on your charity.

SISTER JOANNA OF THE CROSS. Don't say such things!

TERESA. Yes, I must say them. On your charity, on your alms —like a poor beggar and an outcast. I don't mind saying it nor thinking it, for I have been so happy here—yes, I am happy now —happier than the daughter of a king: for I love you all so much that I want to kiss even the walls and hug the trees, for even the walls and the trees have been kind to me. This has been the Convent of my Heart!

SISTER MARCELLA. It has been your home. If only you had been content to stay in it for ever!

PRIORESS. We must not talk like this. God moves in His own ways.

MISTRESS OF NOVICES. And in all of them His children may do His service.

VICARESS. The child was not born to be a religious. The things of the world appeal to her too strongly.

TERESA. It is true. The world appeals to me—poor me! It seems sometimes as if everybody loved me, as if everything was calling to me everywhere to come. I have been so happy in this house, and yet, all the time, I have been thinking how great the world was, how wonderful! Whenever I went out into the street, how my heart leaped! I felt as if I were going to fly, it was so light! My brain was in a whirl. But I was so glad to come back to this house: it felt so tender, as if you were all taking me up in your arms again, as if I had fallen asleep there, warm and sheltered, folded beneath everlasting wings.

VICARESS. The wings of your good angel, who stood waiting at the door—stood waiting till you came.

PRIORESS. Why should he have to wait? Her good angel

always has gone with her, and surely there never has been a time when he has had to turn away his face. Am I right, daughter?
TERESA. You are, Mother. (*Sincerely.*)
SISTER JOANNA OF THE CROSS. They needn't have asked her that!
SISTER MARÍA JESÚS (*rising*). Here are the bows for the corset covers. Do you want them pinned or sewed?
SISTER INEZ. Sewed, I say.
SISTER MARÍA JESÚS. Down the middle?
MISTRESS OF NOVICES. Of course, down the middle.
SISTER MARÍA JESÚS. The reason I asked was because in the pattern they are all fastened down the side.
MISTRESS OF NOVICES (*bending over to examine the fashion plates with* SISTER INEZ *and* SISTER MARÍA JESÚS). Yes. Don't you see? She is right.
SISTER INEZ. That's funny! But they are pretty that way.
MISTRESS OF NOVICES. I say it's absurd.
SISTER MARÍA JESÚS. What do you think, Mother Crucifixion?
VICARESS. Don't ask me; I don't think. I neither understand nor wish to understand these things—pomp and vanity, artifices of the devil, who, they tell me, is very well acquainted with the dressmakers of Paris, and takes part in their designs and encourages their abbreviations. Take it away, take that paper out of my sight, for it never should have entered this holy house!
SISTER MARCELLA. *Ay*, but we have to know the fashions, Mother!
VICARESS. The fashions! The fashions! Go to hell and you will find the fashions! Any other place would be too far behind.
SISTER MARÍA JESÚS. But you wouldn't want the child married in a dress of the year of the ark, would you?
VICARESS. A pure heart and an upright spirit are what she should be married in, and if that is the case, no one is going to notice whether she has one bow more or less.
SISTER MARCELLA. They say men pay a great deal of attention to such things, Mother Crucifixion.
SISTER MARÍA JESÚS. And we must render unto Caesar the things which are Caesar's, and unto God the things which are God's.
VICARESS. Indeed! So we have philosophers in the house!
SISTER INEZ. Hand me the scissors, if you will. I want to cut off these ends.
SISTER JOANNA OF THE CROSS. Now I think everything is ready to put in the trunk.
PRIORESS. Yes, for the carriage will be waiting.

(TERESA *kneels on the floor beside the trunk. The* NUNS *hand her the various articles of the trousseau, which they remove from the benches and the table.*)

SISTER INEZ. Here are the chemises.

SISTER MARCELLA. And the lace petticoats.
SISTER JOANNA OF THE CROSS. Put them in the other tray, so they won't get wrinkled.
SISTER INEZ. Lord of Mercy! What a tuck! What bungler ran this tuck?
MISTRESS OF NOVICES. You must not say anything against the sister who ran it, Sister; say it would look better if it were re-ironed.
TERESA. But it looks splendid; really it does! Give it to me! Here—let me have them. This is too much trouble for you to take.
PRIORESS. Have you everything?
SISTER MARCELLA. The handkerchiefs?
SISTER JOANNA OF THE CROSS. The dressing-jackets?
VICARESS. Here is some edging that was left over, embroidered by hand. You had better put it in the trunk in case of accident.
MISTRESS OF NOVICES. And the patterns—you might need them.
SISTER INEZ. Here is a sachet, my child. It is filled with thyme and lavender and has lime peel in it. It will give a fresh scent to your clothes.
SISTER MARCELLA. She'll have real perfumes soon enough.
SISTER MARÍA JESÚS. Yes, expensive ones.
SISTER INEZ. They may be more expensive, but they won't be any better—I can tell you that; for these are plants that God has made, and they smell sweetly, and of a good conscience. I have them in all the presses in the sacristy, and it is a joy to smell them when you go up the steps to the altar.
TERESA. I think we have everything.
PRIORESS. Yes, everything. Now turn the key. Does it lock securely?

(TERESA *gets up*.)

And hang the key around your neck with the rosaries, for we have fastened it on a ribbon for you. Take care you don't lose it. The lock is an English one, and not every key will open it.
TERESA. Yes, Mother.
VICARESS. It will be a miracle if she has it to-morrow.
SISTER JOANNA OF THE CROSS. She will soon settle down under the responsibilities of a wife.
MISTRESS OF NOVICES. Well? Are you satisfied?
TERESA. Satisfied is too little, Mother. It does not express it. I don't deserve what you have done for me.
VICARESS. Yes, you do; you deserve it. And you might as well tell the truth as a falsehood. You have a good heart; you are a sensible girl. When you said what you did, you were thinking of your clothes; but you need have no scruples. Everything that you take away with you from this house, and more too, you have earned by your labour. That is the truth and you know it. Maybe we have taught you how to sew and embroider, but you have worked

Act II.]   THE CRADLE SONG.   41

for us in the convent, and outside of it. You owe us nothing. Besides, you had two hundred and fifty pesetas from the Doctor to buy the material. Here (*producing a paper from under her scapular*) is the account of the way they have been spent, so you can see for yourself and answer for it, since delicacy will not permit that we should be asked how it was used.

TERESA (*embarrassed and confused*). What do you mean ? Why, Mother Crucifixion !

VICARESS. That is all there is to it. You will find the account is correct.

(TERESA *takes the paper and, having folded it, puts it in her dress.*)

PRIORESS (*to the* NUNS *who have been working*). You may remove the table and gather up these things.

TERESA. No, Mother—let me do it. I will pick up everything.

(*The* PRIORESS *makes a sign and all the* NUNS *rise and leave the room, except herself, the* VICARESS, *the* MISTRESS OF NOVICES, *and* SISTER JOANNA OF THE CROSS.)

PRIORESS (*to* TERESA). What time do you go ?

TERESA. My father is coming for me at five. But before I go, Antonio asked me to say that he would like to see you, to tell you all how happy you have made him and how grateful he is to you for the little girl you have brought up.

PRIORESS. We shall be very glad to see him.

VICARESS. Glad or not glad, no matter; it is our obligation. He cannot expect to carry her off like a thief in the night, and have no woman ask a question.

TERESA. I will call you when he comes.

(*The* PRIORESS, VICARESS *and the* MISTRESS OF NOVICES *go out.* TERESA *and* SISTER JOANNA OF THE CROSS *remain behind, picking up and arranging the papers, patterns and scraps that have been left on the seats or about the floor. They say nothing but presently* TERESA *throws herself on her knees before the* NUN.)

TERESA. Sister Joanna of the Cross !

SISTER JOANNA OF THE CROSS. What do you want, my child ?

TERESA. Now that we are alone, bless me while there is no one here to see—no, not one—for you are my Mother, more than all the rest !

SISTER JOANNA OF THE CROSS. Get up.

(TERESA *gets up.*)

Don't talk like that ! We are all equal in God's house.

TERESA. But in my heart you are the first. You mustn't be angry at what I say. How can I help it ? Is it my fault, though I have struggled against it all my life, that I have come to love you so ?

SISTER JOANNA OF THE CROSS. Yes, you have struggled. You have been wilful—— (*Then seeking at once to excuse her.*) But it was because you were strong and well. When a child is silent and keeps to herself in a corner, it is a sign that she is sick or thinking of some evil. But you——

TERESA. *Ay*, Mother! Where do you suppose that I came from?

SISTER JOANNA OF THE CROSS. From Heaven, my daughter, as all of us have come.

TERESA. Do you really think that we have all come from Heaven?

SISTER JOANNA OF THE CROSS. At least you have come from Heaven to me. You say that I am your mother more than the rest; I don't know—it may be. But I know that for years you have been all my happiness and joy.

TERESA. Mother!

SISTER JOANNA OF THE CROSS. I was so glad to hear you laugh and see you run about the cloisters! It was absurd, but when you first came into the Convent and I was about the same age as you are now, I felt for years that it was I who was scampering and playing. And it seemed as if I was a child again and had just begun to live. You were so little, so busy—yes, you were—but I was busy too, if you only knew, before I entered here, at home in our house in the village. I was always singing and dancing, although we were very poor. My mother went out every day to wash in the river or to do housework—she had so many children!—and I was always carrying one about in my arms. And when I entered here, as I could do, thanks to some good ladies, who collected the money for my dowry—God reward them for it—although I had a real vocation, I was sorrowful and homesick thinking of my little brothers and sisters! How I used to cry in the dark corners, and I never dared to say a word! Then the Mother told me that if my melancholy didn't leave me she would be obliged to send me home. And then you came and I forgot everything! That is why I say you came to me from Heaven. And I don't want you to think I am angry, or ashamed—or that it has ever given me a moment's pain to have loved you.

TERESA. Is that the reason that you scold me so?

SISTER JOANNA OF THE CROSS. When have I ever scolded you?

TERESA. Oh, so many times! But no matter. I always tell Antonio, Sister Joanna of the Cross is my mother. She is my mother, my real mother! So now he always calls you Mother whenever he speaks of you.

SISTER JOANNA OF THE CROSS. My daughter, will you be happy with him?

TERESA. Of course! I am sure I will. He is so good and so happy! He says he doesn't know where all his happiness comes from, because his father, who is dead, was mournful as a willow tree, and his mother—the poor lady burst out crying whenever anything good happened to her. How do you suppose she ever managed to have such a boy? Perhaps sad mothers have happy children; what do you think?

SISTER JOANNA OF THE CROSS. How do I know?

TERESA. It must be that way. The first boy I have is going to be—what is the solemnest thing in the world? No, the first is going to be an architect, like his father; but the second can be a missionary, and go to China if he wants to, and convert the heathen. Just think what it would be to have a son who was a saint! I shouldn't have to be so humble in Heaven, then, should I? I should have influence. And here you are all the time, Sister Joanna of the Cross, praying for me and preparing miracles. So you see I have a good start already.

SISTER JOANNA OF THE CROSS. How you do love to talk!

TERESA. Don't I? Isn't it foolish, Mother? Listen! When you were little did you ever want to be a boy? I did. I used to cry because I thought then that I could have been anything I wanted to be—this, that, I didn't care what it was—Captain-General, Archbishop, yes, Pope, even! Or something else. It used to make me mad to think that because I was a girl I couldn't even be an acolyte. But now, since—well, since I love Antonio, and he loves me, I don't care; it doesn't make any difference any more, because if I am poor and know nothing, he is wise and strong; and if I am foolish and of no account, he is, oh, of so much worth! And if I have to stay behind at home and hide myself in the corner, he can go out into the world and mount, oh, so high—wherever a man can go—and instead of making me envious, it makes me so happy! Ah, Sister Joanna of the Cross, how humble it makes a girl when she truly loves a man!

SISTER JOANNA OF THE CROSS. Do you really love him so much?

TERESA. More than life itself! And that is all too little. Perhaps it is a sin, but I can confess to you. Do you believe we shall meet the people in Heaven we love on earth? Because if I don't meet him there and can't always love him as I do now, even more than I do now——

SISTER JOANNA OF THE CROSS (*interrupting*). Hush! Peace! You mustn't say such things. It is a sin.

TERESA. *Ay*, Sister Joanna of the Cross! How sweet it is to be in love!

SISTER JOANNA OF THE CROSS. But what of him? Does he love you so much?

TERESA. Yes, he loves me. How much, I don't know; but it doesn't matter. What makes me happy is that I love him. But sometimes I have been afraid that the day might come when he will stop loving me, and it makes me sad—but if I ever thought that I could stop loving him, why, I would rather die first. After that, what would there be left to live for?

SISTER JOANNA OF THE CROSS. Ah, my child! To continue in God's love!

TERESA. Do you know how I would like to spend my life?

All of it? Sitting on the ground at his feet, looking up into his eyes, just listening to him talk. You don't know how he can talk. He knows everything—everything that there is to know in the world, and he tells you such things! The things that you always have known yourself, in your heart, and couldn't find the way to say them. Even when he is talking some foreign language that you don't understand, his voice is wonderful. I don't know how to explain it, but it seems as if that voice has been talking to you since the day of your birth—— Not only your ears, but your whole body listens. It is like the air you breathe, and taste, which smells so sweet beneath the tree of paradise out in the garden. Ah, Mother, the first day he said "Teresa"—such a simple thing, just my name—it seemed as if I had never heard it before and when he went away, I ran up and down as if I walked on air, chanting, "Teresa, Teresa, Teresa," over and over to myself, without knowing what I was doing.

SISTER JOANNA OF THE CROSS. You frighten me, my child.

TERESA. Do I? Why?

SISTER JOANNA OF THE CROSS. Because you love him so. For earthly love seems to me like a flower that we find by the way—a little brightness granted by God to help us pass through life, as we are weak and frail; it is a drop of honey on our daily bread, to be received joyfully and without fear, but we must keep our hearts whole, daughter, for it will surely pass away.

TERESA. It cannot pass away!

SISTER JOANNA OF THE CROSS. It may; and then what will be left to your soul, if you have set your all on this delight, and it has passed away?

TERESA (*humbly*). You mustn't be angry with me, Mother. No! Look at me! It isn't wrong, I know. Loving him, I—he is so good, so good—it cannot pass away!

SISTER JOANNA OF THE CROSS. Is he a good Christian?

TERESA. He is good, Sister.

SISTER JOANNA OF THE CROSS. But does he fear God?

TERESA. One day he said to me: "I love you because you know how to pray." Don't you see? And another time: "I feel a devotion toward you as toward some holy thing." Devotion toward me! And whenever I think of that, it seems as if I were growing better, suddenly capable of all there is to do and to suffer out in the world, just to know that he will always feel like that!

SISTER JOANNA OF THE CROSS. I hear some one in the parlour. Draw the curtains.

(TERESA, *pulling the cord, draws the curtains over the windows, shutting off the light. The fore part of the stage remains in shadow, but the outer parlour is brightly illuminated.* ANTONIO *has entered and may be seen by* TERESA *and the* NUN *through the crack where the curtains join. He is twenty-five years of age, well-built, manly and*

Act II.] THE CRADLE SONG.

sensitive of feature. He remains alone and his footsteps may be heard on the boards as he paces nervously up and down.)

TERESA (*in a low voice, going up to the* NUN). Yes. It is he.
SISTER JOANNA OF THE CROSS (*seizing her hand*). Ah! How tall he is!
THERESA. Yes, he is tall. And doesn't he look splendid?
SISTER JOANNA OF THE CROSS. Yes, he does. Has he golden hair?
TERESA. No, it's the light; his hair is dark brown, and his eyes are between violet and blue. It's too bad you can't see them. They are so beautiful! When he talks, they sparkle.
SISTER JOANNA OF THE CROSS. How old is he?
TERESA. Just twenty-five.

(ANTONIO *crosses from one side to the other, and continues to pace back and forth.*)

SISTER JOANNA OF THE CROSS. He seems to be of a very active disposition.
TERESA. That is because he is impatient. Shall I speak to him and tell him you are here?
SISTER JOANNA OF THE CROSS (*falling back*). No!
TERESA. Why not? He loves you dearly. (*In a low voice, going up to the grille.*) Good afternoon, Antonio.
ANTONIO (*looking about from one side to the other, unseen*). Teresa? Where are you?
TERESA (*laughing*). Here, lad, here, behind the grille. It is easy to see you are not accustomed to calling on nuns.
ANTONIO. Can't you run back the curtain?
TERESA. No, because I am not alone. Can't you guess who is with me? My Mother.
ANTONIO. Sister Joanna of the Cross?
TERESA (*to the* NUN, *delighted because he has guessed it*). There! Do you see? (*To* ANTONIO.) Sister Joanna of the Cross—exactly. We have been watching you through the grille, and she says that she thinks you are a very handsome young man.
SISTER JOANNA OF THE CROSS. Goodness gracious! You mustn't pay any attention to what she says.
TERESA. Don't be angry, Mother. I think so myself.
ANTONIO. You never told me that before.
TERESA. That is because in here, where you can't see me, I'm not so embarrassed to tell you. Listen! We have to send in word now that you are here; but I want you to tell my Mother something first, for if you stand there like a blockhead without opening your mouth, I am going to be very much ashamed, considering the time I have spent in singing your praises.
ANTONIO. What do you want me to tell her?
TERESA. What you have in your heart.

ANTONIO. But I don't know whether it is proper to tell it to a religious, although it is in my heart, for I love her dearly.

TERESA. Ah! I tell her that a million times a day.

ANTONIO. Then let us tell her together and make it two million; because you must know, Madam, that it is impossible to know Teresa without loving you.

TERESA. This Mother of mine is indeed a treasure!

SISTER JOANNA OF THE CROSS. For shame, my child! (*Blushing, to* ANTONIO.) I also have a great affection for you, sir, for this child has been teaching me to love you. She is a little blind, perhaps, and trusting, for that is natural. She knows nothing of the world, and we—how were we to teach her? And now you are going to take her far away; but don't take her heart away from us, sir, and break ours, when we let go her hand.

ANTONIO. Madam, I swear to you now that I shall always kneel in reverence before the tenderness and virtue which you have planted in her soul.

TERESA. I told you that he was very good, Mother.

SISTER JOANNA OF THE CROSS. May God make you both very happy. And may God remain with you, for his handmaid must go now and seek the Mother.

ANTONIO. But you are coming back?

SISTER JOANNA OF THE CROSS. With the sisters—— Yes, I think so. Good-bye. I have been so happy to know you.

(SISTER JOANNA OF THE CROSS *goes out, greatly moved.* TERESA *remains standing by the grille until the* NUN *has disappeared, without speaking a word.*)

ANTONIO. Now you can draw back the curtain.

TERESA. Yes, a little. (*She runs back the curtain a little way.*) But it won't do you any good, because you won't be able to see me. Do you really like my Mother? Do you really? Why are you so silent? What are you thinking about?

ANTONIO. I don't know; it is very strange. Since I have come into this room, since I have heard your Mother speak, and have heard you, behind this grille, without knowing for certain where you were in the dark, I have been almost afraid to love you. But ah —how I do love you!

TERESA. I like that better.

ANTONIO. Teresa!

TERESA. What is it?

ANTONIO. Will you never forget, will you always carry with you this peace and calm, wherever you go?

TERESA. With you, Antonio?

ANTONIO. Yes, into the world, beyond these walls; for in the world we make so much useless noise. And you—I see it now— you are the mistress of peace and of calm.

TERESA (*laughing*). I the mistress of calm? As if I hadn't been a little flyaway all my life, without an idea in my head! Mother Crucifixion says that since I was passed in on the wheel there hasn't been one moment in this house of what the rules call "profound calm." I know I don't talk much when I am with you—we have been together such a little while, and it has been all too short to listen to you; but you will see when I grow bolder and am not afraid. You will have to put cotton in your ears then. Ah, Antonio! Only think, we are going to have all our lives to be together and listen to each other talk and tell each other things— that is, all our lives for you to tell me things, because I—you will find out soon enough. Tell me really, truly, Antonio: aren't you going to be awfully ashamed to have such an ignorant wife?

ANTONIO. Ignorant or learned?

TERESA. I? Learned? In what?

ANTONIO. In a science which I did not know, and which you have taught to me.

TERESA. You are joking.

ANTONIO. I am in earnest. Until I met you I knew nothing; I did not even know myself.

TERESA. Pshaw!

ANTONIO. You mustn't laugh. Did it ever seem to you, Teresa, that our soul was like a palace?

TERESA. Of course it is! It is like a castle. Santa Teresa says so: The soul is like a castle—the interior of a castle, all made of one diamond above and below. And it has seven courts, and in the last is stored a great treasure——

ANTONIO. Then in the innermost chamber of my soul was stored the love I have for you, and if you had not come and opened the door yourself, and helped me to find it, I should have passed all my life in ignorance, without knowing anything was there.

TERESA. Don't repeat such heresies! Hush! They are coming.

(TERESA *falls back from the grille, after first drawing the curtains again. The* NUNS *in single file enter silently, the youngest first, followed at last by the* MISTRESS OF NOVICES, *the* VICARESS *and the* PRIORESS. *The* PRIORESS *seats herself in the armchair at the* L. *of the grille; the* VICARESS *and the* MISTRESS OF NOVICES *in two other chairs at the* R. *The remaining* NUNS *stand or are seated round about.* TERESA *supports herself with her hand on the back of the* PRIORESS'S *chair.* SISTER JOANNA OF THE CROSS *approaches her and takes her by the other hand. There is absolute silence as the* NUNS *enter and find their places. They look at each other with expectant attention and some nod and smile among themselves. When they are seated, there follows an interval of further silence.*)

PRIORESS. *Ave Maria Purissima!*

(ANTONIO, *somewhat embarrassed, and endeavouring vainly to penetrate the darkness behind the grille, does not answer. The* PRIORESS, *after waiting a moment, turns her head and smiles indulgently at the community.*)

Good afternoon, young man.

ANTONIO. Good afternoon, Madam—or Madams—for behind the mystery of this screen, it is impossible for me to see whether I am speaking with one or with many.

(*The* NUNS *smile quietly and discreetly.*)

PRIORESS (*in a low voice*). Run back the curtain, Sister Inez.

(*The* SISTER *runs back the curtain.*)

You are speaking with the entire community, which takes great pleasure in knowing you.

ANTONIO. Ladies, the pleasure and the honour are mine, and they are much greater than you will be ready to imagine.

SISTER INEZ. Bless us! But isn't he a polite and polished talker?

SISTER TORNERA. Be silent! I want to hear what he has to say.

ANTONIO. I have greatly desired to visit you for a long time. Teresa knew this, and she must have told you.

PRIORESS. That is true. She has indeed. And we have greatly appreciated your desire.

ANTONIO. But the first time I came here it was Advent and the next time Lent; and then Teresa said it was impossible for me to see you.

VICARESS. Clearly. In seasons of penitence we receive no visitors.

ANTONIO. But now it is May and past Easter time.

MISTRESS OF NOVICES. How well acquainted he is with the calendar! Surely you must be very devout, sir.

ANTONIO. I am, madam—very; but chiefly in the worship of certain saints who as yet are not on the altars.

SISTER INEZ. What a nice compliment! Saints, did he say? (*Laughing.*) He *is* a polished talker.

ANTONIO. Ladies, a hundred years hence they will be lighting candles to you, invoking you in their prayers and bring you thank-offerings of crutches and wooden legs in fervent gratitude.

SISTER TORNERA (*laughing*). Does he think we are going to be the patrons of rheumatism?

MISTRESS OF NOVICES. After a hundred years? You are giving us a century of Purgatory.

ANTONIO. No, madam, by all that is holy! I am giving you a century of life, and entrance thereafter directly into the choir of seraphim.

PRIORESS. I fear you speak frivolously, Señor Don Antonio.

ANTONIO. Madam, I was never more earnest in my life. Whenever I think of death, you have no idea of the peace which enters my soul. I remember how many saintly white hands will be stretched down to help me into Paradise—for I suppose that you will be able to exercise a little influence on behalf of one of the family.

SISTER SAGRARIO (*laughing*). One of the family?

VICARESS. Certainly. We are all God's children.

ANTONIO. But I shall be so in a double sense; first, in my own birthright, and then as your son-in-law, who are his brides.

VICARESS. Ah! It is not meet to jest about holy things.

ANTONIO. You are right, madam, and pardon all the foolish things I have said, for I swear they are the outcome of nervousness and fear.

MISTRESS OF NOVICES. You are not afraid of us?

ANTONIO. I am, madam, very—because of the respect and admiration in which I hold you all. I came here more disturbed than ever I have been before in my whole life. I do not know whether I should thank you, or whether I should beg your pardon.

PRIORESS. Beg our pardon?

ANTONIO. Yes, because I fear that I am not worthy of the treasure which you are entrusting to me.

PRIORESS. We know already from the Doctor that you are an honourable young man.

MISTRESS OF NOVICES. And the love which our daughter bears you is our guarantee. Surely the Lord would not permit His child, brought up in His fear, to throw herself away upon an evil man.

ANTONIO. I am not evil, no; but I am a man, and you, ladies, with all the great piety of your souls, have been nurturing a flower for the skies. When I first knew her, my heart whispered that I had met a saint. She was a miracle. An unnatural fear and trembling overcame me when I first dared speak to her; and when I told her of my love, my heart stopped beating and bade me fall on my knees, and now that I have come to you to beg my happiness, I don't know what I can promise in token of my gratitude, nor how to thank you enough for the great honour you have done me.

VICARESS. It may be you are speaking more truly than you think, Señor Don Antonio.

MISTRESS OF NOVICES. Why, Mother!

VICARESS. No, let me speak. For he has said well. The girl is not one of those worldly creatures who take to their husbands a great store of physical beauty. That is certain. You cannot call her ugly, but it is the most that can be said. Nor does she bring with her any dower. She is poorer than the poor. But she carries in her heart a treasure, the only one which we have been able to give her, which is more priceless than silver or gold, and that is the fear of God. For this, sir, you must be answerable to us, and we ask you your word now, that you will always respect it in her and in her children, if it should be God's holy will you should have any.

D

ANTONIO. Teresa shall always be the absolute mistress of her conscience and of my house, and my children will always be as she desires them to be. I pledge my word.

PRIORESS. You will never have reason to regret it, for she is a good and prudent girl.

VICARESS. And not hypocritical, for, although, as you have said, we have nurtured her for the skies, we have never permitted ourselves to believe that she was to reach them through the cloister.

SISTER MARÍA JESÚS. Do you mean to take her very far away?

ANTONIO. Yes, madam. Though there is no longer far or near in the modern world. We sail next week. I am going to America as the resident director of a firm of architects.

PRIORESS. Yes, we know already.

ANTONIO. That is the reason for this haste. I do not wish to go alone.

SISTER TORNERA. Aren't you afraid the child will be seasick? They say you do get a terrible shaking-up upon the sea.

SISTER MARÍA JESÚS. You must promise us to take good care of her.

SISTER INEZ. If she gets overheated never let her drink cold water. She is very pig-headed about that.

SISTER MARCELLA. But you mustn't forget that she is accustomed to cold baths.

SISTER INEZ. If she takes cold or gets a cough, make her drink a glass of hot milk with a teaspoonful of hot rum in it, and plenty of sugar, for that's the only thing that will make her sweat.

TERESA. I think perhaps I had better attend to these matters myself, Sister.

SISTER INEZ. Yes, you'd be a pretty one to attend to them! Take no notice of what she says, Señor Don Antonio: she is quite spoiled. When you give her medicines, you have to force the spoon into her mouth; she might be dying, but she would never ask for anything herself!

PRIORESS. We had better not confuse him with too many recommendations. Surely he knows the more important precautions already.

ANTONIO (*smiling*). Perhaps it would be better if you wrote them out for me on a piece of paper.

SISTER TORNERA. A good idea! (*Laughing.*) If we began, where does he think we'd leave off?

SISTER SAGRARIO. How many days will you be on the ship?

ANTONIO. Two weeks.

SISTER MARCELLA. Mercy! What an age! Suppose there should be a storm?

MISTRESS OF NOVICES. It will be at least two weeks more before we can get letters back.

ANTONIO. We will telegraph when we arrive and we will send

you a message from the middle of the ocean, so that you will hear from us the same day.

TERESA. Words flying through the air, like birds.

SISTER INEZ. What will men invent next? When your handmaid was in the world, they came by a wire, and yet it seemed the work of the devil.

ANTONIO. I should not advise you to believe that the devil is ever very far away from such inventions, madam.

SISTER INEZ. Whether he is or not, when the telegram comes it will be safest to sprinkle it with holy water.

PRIORESS. Ah, Sister Inez, you are so simple! Don't you see that the young man is only joking?

VICARESS. It is five o'clock—the hour we were to expect your father.

ANTONIO. I do not wish to molest you further.

PRIORESS. You do not molest us, but we must close the parlour at five.

ANTONIO. You will pardon me if I commit a breach of etiquette, but I should like to ask you one favour before I go.

PRIORESS. If it is in our power to grant——

ANTONIO. Although it seems you have drawn a curtain, yet the mystery of this screen is as inscrutable as ever to a poor sinner like myself; and I should be sorry to go away without having seen you face to face. Is it too much to ask?

PRIORESS. For us this is a day of giving. Draw back the curtains, Teresa.

(TERESA *draws back the curtain from one window, a* NUN *that from the other, lighting up the room.*)

ANTONIO (*bowing*). Ladies!

VICARESS. Well? How does the vision appear to you?

ANTONIO. I shall never forget it as long as I live.

PRIORESS. Then may God go with you, and may you live a thousand years. (*Taking* TERESA *by the hand.*) Here is her hand. See, we give her to you with a great love, and may you make her happy.

ANTONIO. I answer for her happiness with my life.

PRIORESS. And may God go with you.

MISTRESS OF NOVICES. Teresa will give you from us two scapularies, the remembrances of a nun. They are not worth anything, but they have lain beside the reliquary of our father, the Blessed Saint Dominic. Keep them in memory of this day.

ANTONIO. I shall treasure them, ladies, from this hour. And I pray you, always remember me in your prayers.

VICARESS. For your part, do not forget to pray with them from time to time, for although everyone has power to help our souls toward Heaven, we must take the first steps ourselves. And may God go with you.

ALL. God go with you.
ANTONIO. Ladies!

(*He retires and disappears. A* NUN *draws the curtain over the grille. Then a moment's silence. Some of the* NUNS *sigh and say :*)

NUNS. Ah, Lord! Good Lord! May it be God's holy will!

(*The bell by the door rings twice.*)

VICARESS. I thought so—your father.

(TERESA *stands in the midst of the group of* NUNS, *bewildered, looking from one to the other, greatly moved.* SISTER TORNERA *goes to open the door.*)

PRIORESS. Ask him to come in.

(*The* DOCTOR *enters on the arm of* SISTER TORNERA. *He is now very old, but neither decrepit nor cast down.*)

DOCTOR. Good afternoon, ladies; good afternoon, daughter.
TERESA (*kissing his hand*). Good afternoon, Father.
DOCTOR. The whole assembly—the parting, eh? Well, did you see the young man? (*The* NUNS *do not answer.*) A fine fellow, isn't he? He is waiting outside. We have an hour in the coach before we arrive at the station, so you had better get ready now, daughter.

(TERESA *goes out with* SISTER JOANNA OF THE CROSS.)

Ah! The trunk? Good! Carry it to the door. The boys outside will take care of it.

(*Two* NUNS *lift the trunk and carry it out.*)

There, that is done. (*He seats himself in the* PRIORESS'S *chair.*) Well, how are we to-day?
PRIORESS. You see, Doctor.
MISTRESS OF NOVICES. Who would ever have believed it eighteen years ago?
DOCTOR. Eighteen years? We are growing old, Mother. We are growing old.
PRIORESS. That is not the worst of it.
SISTER INEZ. How old are you now, Doctor?
DOCTOR. Seventy-eight, Sister.
SISTER INEZ. No one would ever think it.
DOCTOR (*attempting a witticism so as to cheer up the* NUNS). That is because I am preserved in sanctity, like a fly in thick syrup. (*But none of the* NUNS *laugh.*) A little mournful to-day, eh?
SISTER MARCELLA. What else did you expect?
SISTER SAGRARIO. She is not even going to be married in our chapel.

Act II.] THE CRADLE SONG. 53

DOCTOR. No, his mother is old and sick, and naturally she wants him to be with her, so they must be married in her house.
PRIORESS. Naturally. Poor woman!

(*A pause.*)

MISTRESS OF NOVICES. She is going so far away!
DOCTOR. But she will come back, Mother. She will come back.
PRIORESS. She knows nothing of the world.
DOCTOR. There is no cause to be alarmed. He is an honourable man.
VICARESS. Yes, so it would seem.

(TERESA *and* SISTER JOANNA OF THE CROSS *re-enter. It is plain that they have both been crying.* TERESA, *wearing a mantilla, and with her coat on, carries a shawl over her arm for use as a wrap on the voyage. She stops in the middle of the room and stands still, not daring to say good-bye.*)

DOCTOR. Well? Are we ready now?
TERESA. Yes—— Now——
DOCTOR. Then say good-bye. It is late. We must be going, daughter.
PRIORESS. Yes, you must not delay.
TERESA (*throwing herself on her knees before the* PRIORESS, *and kissing her scapular*). Mother!
PRIORESS. Rise, my daughter, rise.
TERESA. Bless me, Mother! Bless me!
PRIORESS. May God bless you; so. Rise.

(*As* TERESA *rises, the* NUN *embraces her.*)

TERESA. Mother! I don't know what to say to you—I don't know how to leave you—but you must forgive me all the wrong I have ever done in all these years. I have been foolish, wilful. I have given you all so much trouble you must forgive me. I would like to do something great and splendid for all of you. But—but may God reward you! May God reward you! God reward you! (*She bursts into tears.*)
PRIORESS. My daughter, come! You must not cry. You must now allow yourself to be so afflicted.
TERESA. I am not afflicted, Mother; but—it's—Mother, I can never forget you! You must pray for me, pray for me! And you must never forget me!
PRIORESS. Ah, no, my child! Never! We will pray God to help you, and to be with you, and you must pray to Him for guidance and for counsel always, whenever you are troubled or perplexed in anything. For the liberty which they enjoy in the world is like a sword in the hands of a child, and life at best is hard, and bitter often-times.
MISTRESS OF NOVICES. Be thankful that your heart is well

steeled to resist all the temptations that may come. Is it not, my daughter?

TERESA. It is, Mother.

PRIORESS. Will you promise always to be reverent and good?

TERESA. Yes! Yes, Mother!

VICARESS. Remember that your obligation is greater than that of others, because you have come forth from God's own house.

TERESA. Yes! Yes, Mother!

PRIORESS. Remember all the blessings He has showered upon you from the cradle; remember that your whole life has been as a miracle, that you have lived here as few have ever lived, that you have been brought up as few have ever been brought up, like the Holy Virgin herself, in the very temple of the Lord.

MISTRESS OF NOVICES. As He was to the Evangelist, so God has been to you a father and a mother, more than to any other living thing.

PRIORESS. Remember that you are the rose of His garden and the grain of incense upon His altar.

TERESA. Yes! Mother, yes! I will!—— I will remember all —all—all——

MISTRESS OF NOVICES. And do not forget to examine your soul each day.

TERESA. No, Mother.

SISTER JOANNA OF THE CROSS. And write often.

TERESA. Yes, Mother.

DOCTOR. It is time to go, Teresa.

TERESA (*throwing herself suddenly into his arms*). Oh, Father! Promise me never to leave them! Never abandon them!

DOCTOR. Child of my heart! Ah, may they never abandon me! —for this is my house. For more than forty years I have been coming here day by day, hour by hour, and now there is nobody within these walls who is older than I. I have no children. I have had my loves—yes, a moment's flame—but it was so long ago! I have forgotten them. And these Sisters, who have been mothers to you, have been daughters to me; and now, when I come, they no longer even cover their faces before me. Why should they? It seems to me as if I had seen them born. (*Greatly moved.*) And I should like to die in this house, so that they may shut my eyes and say a prayer for me when life itself is ended.

MISTRESS OF NOVICES. Who is thinking of dying, Doctor?

PRIORESS. It is time to go.

TERESA (*looking from one to the other*). Aren't you going to embrace me?

(*The* NUNS, *after hesitating and glancing a moment doubtfully at the* MOTHER PRIORESS, *embrace* TERESA *in turn, in perfect silence. Only* SISTER JOANNA OF THE CROSS, *taking her into her arms, says :*)

SISTER JOANNA OF THE CROSS. My child!

Act II.]   THE CRADLE SONG.

PRIORESS. May you find what you seek in the world, daughter, for so we hope and so we pray to God. But if it should not be so, remember, this is your Convent.

TERESA. Thanks—thanks—— (*Sobbing.*)

DOCTOR. Come, daughter, come——

(*The* DOCTOR *and* TERESA *go to the door, but* TERESA *turns when she reaches the threshold and embraces* SISTER JOANNA OF THE CROSS, *passionately. Then she disappears.* SISTER JOANNA OF THE CROSS *rests her head against the grille, her back to the others, and weeps silently. A pause. The bells of the coach are heard outside as it drives away.*)

MISTRESS OF NOVICES. They are going now.

(*The chapel bell rings summoning the* NUNS *to choir.*)

PRIORESS. The summons to the choir.

MISTRESS OF NOVICES. Come, Sisters! Let us go there.

(*All make ready to go out sadly. The* VICARESS, *sensing the situation, to her mind demoralizing, feels it to be her duty to provide a remedy. She, too, is greatly moved, but making a supreme effort to control herself, says in a voice which she in vain endeavours to make calm but which is choked in utterance by tears :*)

VICARESS. One moment. I have recently observed that in the prayer some of you have not been marking the pauses in the lines sufficiently, while the last words are dragged out interminably. Be careful of this, for your Reverences know that the beauty of the office lies in rightly marking the pauses, and in avoiding undue emphasis on the end of the phrase. Let us go in.

(*The* NUNS *file out slowly.* SISTER JOANNA OF THE CROSS, *unnoticed, remains alone. With a cry, she falls upon her knees beside an empty chair.*)

CURTAIN.

Character costumes and wigs used in the performance of plays contained in French's Acting Edition may be obtained from Messrs CHARLES H. FOX LTD, 184 High Holborn, London, W.C.1.

NOTES ON DIRECTION AND PERFORMANCE

"The Cradle Song" is essentially realistic in conception and execution, a veracious genre-picture of convent life. In acting, therefore, it depends to an unusual degree upon detail, upon the contrast and cumulation of minute effects. In the dialogue every syllable has its value.

PLAY SLOWLY. Allow the audience not only to *get* but to *digest* the points of the dialogue. At the end of every episode and scene, give it a chance to set.

Avoid impressionistic or modernistic effects. They are too broad and violent for the delicate fabric of the play.

Note that the language is Biblical in suggestion, hence reverent and measured, especially in the older nuns.

Simplicity is essential, affectation fatal.

Architectural display will be found particularly injurious. The impression must on no account be created that the Convent is a country estate where the nuns, in antiphonal choirs, chant celestial music.

In the Civic Repertory production the music is restricted to the Compline music at the end of Act I, and TERESA's song in Act II, both unaccompanied.

It is imperative that TERESA possess a pleasing personality. When she appears the audience has already been sated with the Convent routine, and youth, charm and infectious gaiety are demanded.

The principal contrast of the play, that between the world and the cloister, is visualized in ANTONIO's visit. Behind the grille is the full light, in front the darkened stage. To obtain a sudden contrast the curtain over the grille must be opaque, not a mere veil.

ANTONIO's impatient footfalls should be distinctly heard before he is discovered.

Emphasize the exit of the DOCTOR to visit the bed-ridden sister in Act I. If played slowly, the exit of the SISTER preceding him with the warning bell will prove effective.

Stress also the ritual of the wheel.

Upon the VICARESS's complaint that the community has conversed unveiled before the DOCTOR, she alone covers her face. This point, together with her subsequent realization of the fact, will require careful playing.

In Spain the DOCTOR wears a top-hat and black frock-coat, neither of course new. At the Civic Repertory Theatre the hat is soft, the coat brown; he also carries a brown bag. In Act II he wears a black suit and cape.

The POET appears in black. Flowing cape. No hat.

The Interlude should be spoken at stage c. before the Curtain if a dividing curtain is used. Enter and leave at c. Otherwise, the POET speaks at stage B., withdrawing, R., as the Curtain rises.

TERESA's song in Act II, interrupting the reading of the SISTERS, consists of three stanzas. In performance only the words of the first stanza are used, repeated in place of the others at such length and in such order as the pace of the performance renders desirable.

TERESA's final speech to ANTONIO preparatory to the general entrance of the SISTERS reads:

> "Hush! Don't repeat such heresies.
> They are coming——"

In secular performances, it will be found more effective to read simply:

> "Hush! They are coming——"

J. G. U.

GREGORIO AND MARÍA MARTÍNEZ SIERRA

Gregorio Martínez Sierra was born at Madrid March 6, 1881, María de la O Lejárraga at San Millán de la Cogolla, a mountain village in the fertile winegrowing district of the Rioja, one year previously. They were married in 1899. Gregorio Martínez Sierra is both a person and a pen-name, and the works which have appeared as his are the result of a collaboration that began even before marriage and has continued through a prolonged series of books and plays ever since.

Precocious in talent, Gregorio attended the University of Madrid where he came to grief in history, doubtless, as he says, because of a settled aversion to battles. His affinity for formal study was slight. María, however, associated herself with the educational system and early became established as a teacher in the public normal schools. Together they soon abandoned all thought of academic preferment and turned to literature as a career.

At seventeen, with the manuscript of his first book, *El poema del trabajo* ("The Song of Labour"), he presented himself to Jacinto Benavente, who furnished an introduction and arranged its publication which took place in 1898. Two series of prose poems, or pastels, as they were called in that day, followed, besides a collection of short stories, *Cuentos breves*, issued independently and attributed to María. In 1900 a novelette, *Almas ausentes*, was awarded the prize in a contest conducted by the *Biblioteca Mignon*. This and other tales of the sort, subsequently appearing separately, have been reprinted in three volumes, *Abril melancólico* ("Melancholy April"), *El diablo se ríe* ("The Devil Laughs"), and *La selva muda* ("The Silent Wood"). The most notable work in the shorter form, however, is contained in *Sol de la tarde*, or "Declining Sun," which established their reputation beyond cavil in 1904. To the same year belongs the first of two novels, "The Humble Truth," while a second and more popular venture in the field of fiction, "Peace" (*Tú eres la paz*), was composed two years later.

In the beginning an intellectual by temperament and a word-painter by inclination, Martínez Sierra may be characterized as an impressionist, well versed in the procedure of the modern French schools. Perhaps the principal personal influence of his formative period was that of the poet Juan Ramón Jiménez, with whom he kept bachelor hall at Madrid. Other associations of these days were likewise predominantly literary, and the leaders of the modern movement such as Antonio and Manuel Machado and the Catalan, Santiago Rusiñol, painter of gardens, proved themselves kindred spirits. Under their friendly stimulus, he published a volume of verse, *La casa de la primavera*, a chance excursion into an alien domain, as well as a prose poem upon "Hamlet in the Person of Sarah Bernhardt." With these works his "Dream Theatre" may be coupled, a quartet of symbolic, mystical dialogues with pronounced Maeterlinckian tendencies.

The first decade of the productivity of Martínez Sierra suggests little of the theatre. It was quietistic in feeling, essentially contemplative, a communion with idyllic and elegiac poets. Yet through these days another influence had been active, although less conspicuously, which in the end was to prove decisive. In the year immediately following the publication of "The Song of Labour," the Art Theatre was founded at Madrid by Benavente. The co-operation of the more promising of the younger generation was enlisted, among whom was Martínez Sierra, who played the rôle of Manuel in support of Benavente in the latter's comedy "A Long Farewell" at the opening performance. The ensuing months were months of intimate association with a remarkable mind. "As I listened to him talk, the fundamental laws of the modern theatre were revealed to me, and I have profited by his instruction unceasingly." So, properly, Martínez Sierra had already served an apprenticeship in the theatre before he began to write plays. His début as a playwright was delayed for ten years, and was then made in collaboration with Rusiñol, with whom he composed a comedy entitled *Vida y dulzura*, presented at the Teatro de la Comedia, Madrid, in 1907. This was followed by *Aucells de pas*, also in collaboration with Rusiñol, produced in Catalan at Barcelona in 1908, and, after a further interval of two years, by *Cors de dona*, in Catalan by the same hands. Meanwhile, during the spring of 1909, Martínez Sierra attained his first independent success with the comedy in two acts, *La sombra del padre*, presented at the Lara Theatre, one of the favourite houses of the capital. *El ama de la casa* ("The Mistress of the House") was acted at the same theatre in 1910, and in 1911 he achieved a definite and permanent triumph with the production of "The Cradle Song" (*Canción de cuna*). A companion piece, *Los pastores* ("The Two Shepherds"), was brought out in 1913, also at the Lara. As Martínez Sierra's non-dramatic prose becomes most nicely expressive, most pictorial and most imaginative in *Sol de la tarde*, his comedy attains perfection in these beautiful idylls of the religious life. No other plays convey so convincingly, or with equal grace, the implications of environment as it interprets itself in terms of character, not symbolically nor in any didactic way, but directly and visually so that the ambient becomes the protagonist rather than the individual, and the spirit of the *milieu* is felt to express more clearly than words the fundamentals which condition its life.

"The Cradle Song" has been translated into many languages, and has been played and imitated widely throughout the civilized world. Ten years after the Madrid premiere Augustin Duncan hazarded four special matinees in English at the Times Square Theatre, New York, without, however, attracting support. A play in two acts was held to be revolutionary by the consensus of experts, and was thought to fall wholly without the purlieus of drama. During the same season a slighter piece, "The Romantic Young Lady" (*Sueño de una noche de agosto*), reached the London stage with Dennis Eadie, achieving a *succès d'estime*. The publication of the plays in translation fortunately attracted general attention, and it was not long before the wisdom of the pioneers had been justified. "The Lover" met with favour at the Fortune Theatre and on tour through England and Scotland, "Madame Pepita" came to the Play-house, Oxford, and the Festival Theatre, Cambridge. "Love Magic," the first piece by Sierra to be acted in English (Waldorf-Astoria, New York, March, 1918). "Poor John," "The Two Shepherds" and "Wife to a Famous Man" are equally familiar in the little theatres of Great Britain and America. Finally, during the fall of 1927, Miss Scaife and Mr. Eadie brought "The Kingdom of God" to the Strand Theatre, and the same play, staged and directed by Miss Ethel Barrymore, was chosen to inaugurate the new Ethel Barrymore Theatre in New York in December, 1928.

Martínez Sierra has now written more than fifty original plays which have been acted, in addition to the three composed in collaboration with Rusiñol. He has translated and adapted another fifty, chiefly from the French, English and Catalan, besides making occasional excursions into German. Perhaps the most important translation is a five-volume edition of Maeterlinck. His non-dramatic works occupy thirty-two volumes to which six others of translations must be added. In the intervals of composition, he established and edited *Helios*, a short-lived literary periodical, and founded and directed the *Biblioteca Renacimiento*, one of the most prosperous and progressive publishing houses of the capital. He has also edited a library of the world's classics in translation, and more recently he conducted a publishing house of his own, the *Biblioteca Estrella*. In 1916, he assumed the management of the Teatro Eslava, Madrid, installing there a stock company, the *Compañía Lírico-Dramática Gregorio Martínez Sierra*, for the presentation of the modern repertory, prominently featuring his own plays. A Parisian engagement was undertaken successfully in 1925, and the company has since repeatedly visited America, appearing first in a repertory of eighteen plays upon a tour extending from Buenos Aires to New York, terminating at the Forrest Theatre, in May, 1927. An admirably printed and illustrated selection of monographs, *Un teatro de arte en España*, records the story of ten years spent at the Eslava and renders adequate tribute to Catalina Bárcena, the gifted and versatile actress around whom from the beginning the company was built.

An artist who is subjected continually to the distractions of business, sacrifices with his leisure opportunity for detachment. Already, previous to the production of *Los pastores*, Martínez Sierra had manifested a tendency to approximate the main currents of the modern popular theatre. An improviser of unusual facility, he composed the slightest of musical comedies in *Margot* and *La Tirana*; a charming light opera libretto, *Las golondrinas* ("The Swallows"), based upon an earlier play, *Aucells de pas*; grand opera libretto in *La llama*, and the scenario of a dancing suite with music by Manuel de Falla for the gypsy *bailarina* Pastora Imperio. He re-made old comedies, reworked juvenilia, republished forgotten stories, and dramatized his novel *Tú eres la paz* as *Madrigal*. He contrived pantomime. The lesser plays of this miscellaneous epoch become an epitome of the activities of the contemporary Madrid stage, broadened, however, by a thorough cosmopolitanism. They are eclectic, light-hearted, persistently gay, and, upon the more serious side, progressive documents considered from the sociological point of view. Even his *Don Juan de España*, a re-embodiment of the traditional libertine celebrated by Tirso de Molina and by Zorrilla, is a Don Juan redeemed. Later works, perhaps, especially those falling within the post-war period, betray in the main a diminution of social and ethical preoccupation, but reveal increasingly modernistic and expressionistic bias.

The progressive, the modernistic has in fact possessed an extraordinary fascination for both collaborators in the composite personality known as Martínez Sierra. It became articulate in the practical sphere some years since in "Letters to the Women of Spain," "Feminism, Femininity and the Spanish Spirit" and "The Modern Woman," all volumes of confessed propaganda, skilfully couched in a style quite as persuasive and dispassionate as that of the plays. The initiative here may fairly be attributed to María. These books, indeed, contemplated adjustments in the social order sufficiently radical to amount to revolution. When at last economic stress and political unrest combined to precipitate a national crisis, and the revolution became actual, María threw herself into active life, and entered the Cortés, or parliament, where she sits for the City of Granada. Gregorio, meanwhile, has devoted himself to motion pictures.

J. G. U.

ACT 1.

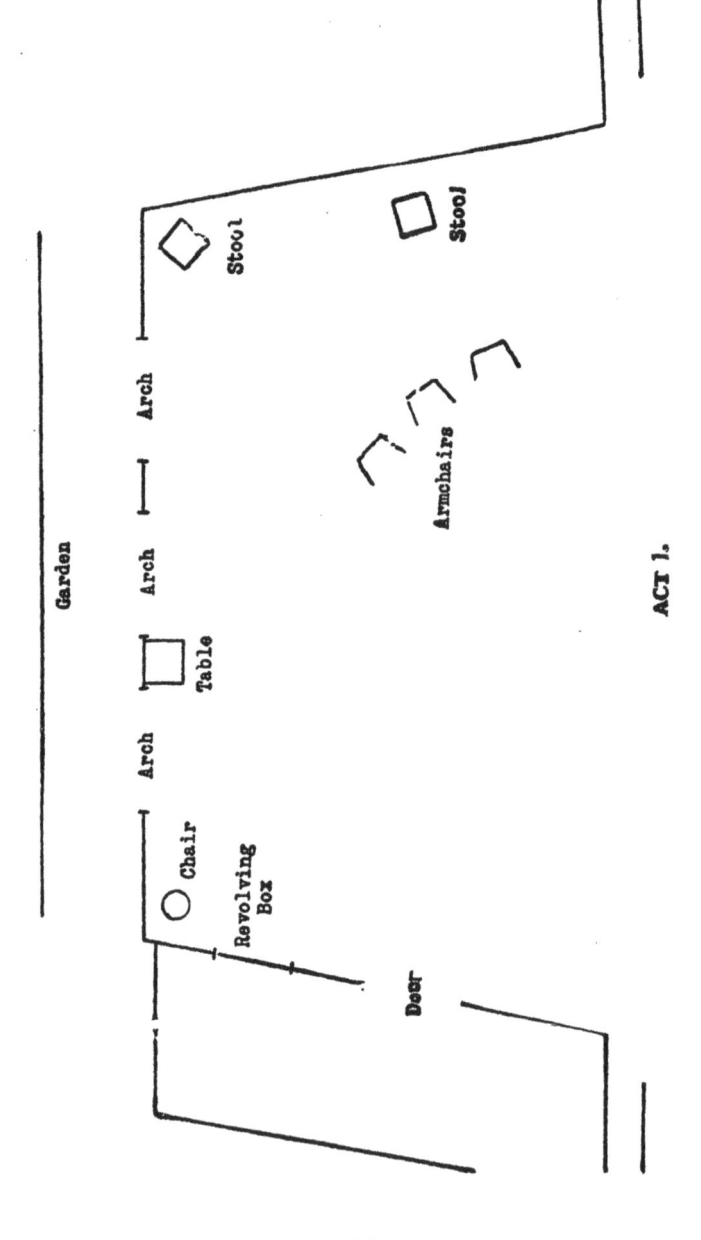

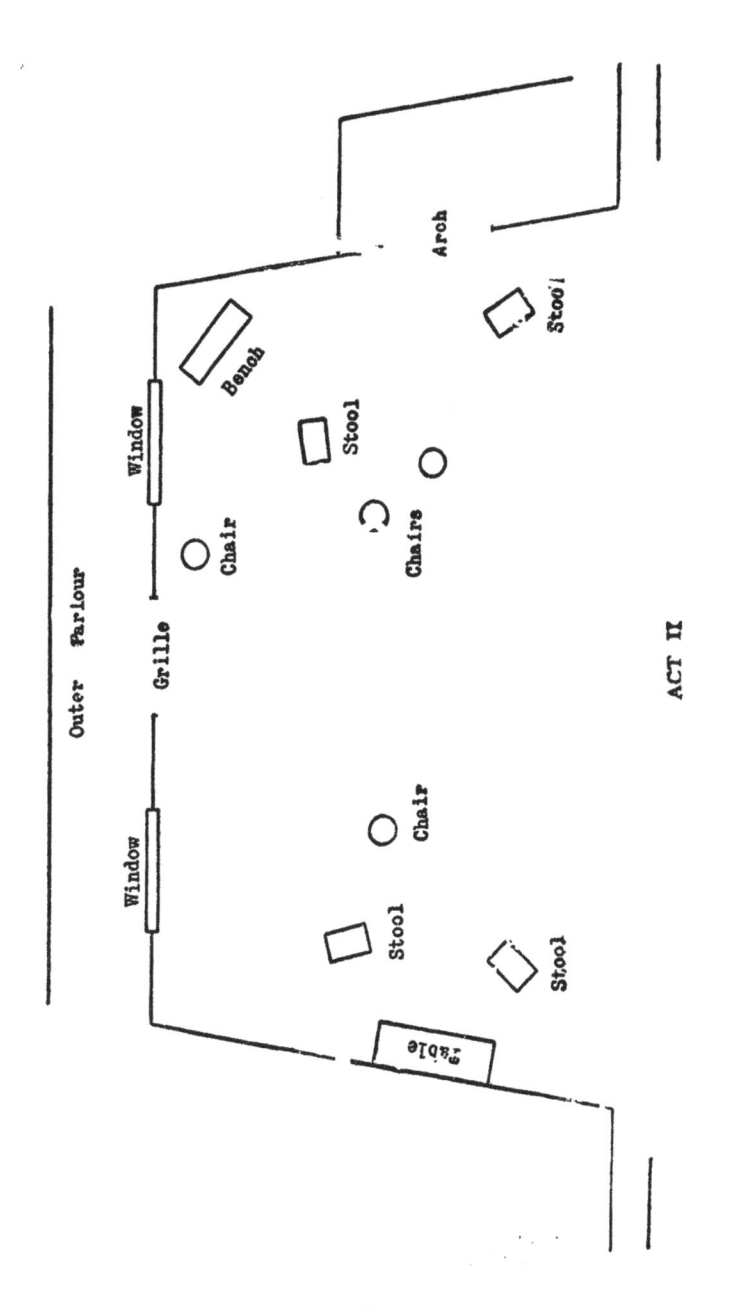

ACT II

Outer Parlour

- Window
- Bench
- Stool
- Chair
- Chairs
- Grille
- Arch
- Stool
- Window
- Stool
- Chair
- Stool
- Table

19